STICKING OUT IN MINNESOTA

First published in 2008 by
Appletree Press Ltd
The Old Potato Station
14 Howard Street South
Belfast BT7 1AP

Tel: +44 (028) 90 24 30 74
Fax: +44 (028) 90 24 67 56
Email: reception@appletree.ie
Web: www.appletree.ie

A catalogue record for this book is
available from the British Library.

Sticking Out in Minnesota – A Dubliner's Journey

ISBN-13: 978 1 84758 107 5

Desk and Marketing Editor: Jean Brown
Copy-Editor: Jim Black
Designer: Stuart Wilkinson
Production Manager: Paul McAvoy

9 8 7 6 5 4 3 2 1

AP3581

STICKING OUT IN MINNESOTA

A Dubliner's Journey

Seán Carabini

Appletree Press

For John, Teresa, Ciarán and Chrissy

CONTENTS

ACKNOWLEDGEMENTS

It is impossible to thank all who helped me in this endeavour. I have selected a few to thank in particular:

To Chrissy, my wife, a real-life Minnesotan, who acted as my sounding board, unofficial editor, and, on the days I had trouble finding my way through the sea of words, my drum-master.

To my parents for their constant support and belief in me.

To my brother, who likes to be thanked.

In America:

To all my American friends and family who both put me up and put up with me, for the experiences we shared that are contained in this book.

Thanks to Liz, Ryan, Lisa and Chris for reading early drafts and giving me helpful feedback. A big friendly wave to the Skeltons, Bergmans (both American and Canadian varieties) and Tokkesdals.

In Ireland:

To all my friends and family who offered me words of advice – particularly Stephen and Kerrie who gave me constructive criticism when needed.

To the team at Appletree – particularly Jean and Jim – who have turned a rough manuscript into a book.

Finally, a big thank you to Minnesota itself. Do I enjoy visiting your state? You Betcha!

PREFACE

As I step off the plane in Minneapolis, the first thing that hits me is the heat. If it's summer, there's too much – if it's winter, there's not enough. It is summer. Plodding bouncily, wearily, down the graded jetway, the heat wraps itself around my shoulders, like burning water. It continues down my spine, and makes the small of my back sweat. My face turns as red as dark, warm blood.

The heat mixes with the exhaustion caused by a day's travel, and hits me in waves of nothingness. One moment, breath labours. The next, I breathe easier, with an eerie awareness – but there is never enough time to be aware of anything much before the next wave hits.

The travel bag slung over my shoulder is soon damp – I am sweating as if my clothing is my skin. A full day now pours from my bloodstream, my forehead glistening and salty, the backs of my knees sticky with ripples of sweat streams. I am hot. It is all I can think about. I carry a hot, wet screaming monkey on my back.

We greet those who have shown up to greet us – damp hugs, tired broken smiles, kisses like sea-salt. We collect our luggage, and make for the open-air parking lot.

It is never a pleasure to step outside, for there is no respite. Inside, I could *feel* it. Now, I can *smell* it. A thousand beating summer's days balance heavily and precariously like hard, soggy water around my neck. I am engulfed. It is too hot. It is more than my Irish body can take. And the smell – the smell. The aroma of scorch wafts drearily through my nostrils. My nose labours to breathe – the air is a hundred times heavier than back home.

People are poorly dressed – all cotton, all grey. It is too hot to care. We get into the car, sinking into melting seats. It is darker inside – a dull heat that bores into my very being. I am overwhelmed. It is too hot.

I strike up a conversation about the flight – each word, a thousand times heavier than it is in Dublin, thuds forth in search of a receptive ear. The road is littered with these verbal boulders – the leaden air crashing to the ground, unable to support words themselves.

By the time we reach our destination, the car seat beneath me has gone from damp to wet to hot and sodden. I pull on a very warm door handle. The door pops open. I seek relief from the heat of the car. It does not come. Once again, stepping out into the baking Minnesota air, I seek respite. There is none.

I sought relief. There was none. Now, not knowing what else to seek, I seek forgiveness.

INTRODUCTION

People don't travel to find out more about the world. That's called 'emigration'. People travel to be reminded about where they come from and, ultimately, to be told who they are. Travelling allows others to point out our cultural layers to us and, thus, brings us a little closer to the individual beneath the layers.

Culture is the array of ways that we do things 'right'. When we travel, we learn that what we thought of as 'right' back home tends to be 'wrong' – as opposed to 'different' - in other places.

This book describes my journey, or, rather, a series of journeys – as a Dubliner – through Minnesota – a part of America in which I am perpetually 'wrong'. In the following pages, I share the stories and anecdotes that have shaped my relationship with the phenomenon that is 'America'. Ultimately, these are the stories through which I discovered (and continue to discover) myself, who I am and how I react in different situations.

My stories are not at all atypical – those of a 'Post-student' trying to figure out his place in the world with little money and less influence. I travelled for the same reason as millions before me – a woman! Before meeting her, I had little desire to ever visit Minnesota – or America at all, for that matter.

When I first went to Minnesota, I knew little or nothing about it. I had read a little about how its 'small-town meets big-city' cultural frame had provided the setting from which icons such as Prince, Bob Dylan and Judy Garland on one hand and Laura Ingalls Wilder's 'Little House on the Prairie' on the other had emerged. I surmised that the local sense of humour might have been captured by the *Peanuts* cartoon strip, by the Minnesotan character 'Rose' from the *Golden Girls* and by the literary works of Garrison Keillor. What I hadn't yet fully discovered, however, was my own identity – that of a Dubliner – the backdrop against which I would interact with the world.

Minnesota challenged me to understand myself first and foremost. And only once I had discovered my own Dublin roots was I able to understand Minnesota.

More than anything, this book records the conversation that Minnesota and myself have been engaged in for the past eight years.

CHAPTER ONE

America from a Distance

I awake with a hangover, having spent the night at a friend's studio apartment in Rathmines, Dublin. It had been an interesting evening. Some wanker called Ciaran from Cork had crashed our little party and thought it would be really funny to knock on every door in the building at 2.00 a.m., leaving screaming babies and angry, tired fathers in his wake. We got our own back, though. We plied him with alcohol, until his speech was neither coherent nor functional. When each of his eyes began to focus on different things – the left on sleep, the right on wakefulness, we knew it was time. We lay him down on the floor, and took out a selection of shoe polishes, permanent markers and ballpoint pens. Duncan drew a pirate moustache and patch on his face. I removed his top and drew a bra on him in heavy permanent marker. A girl, whose name I've forgotten, practiced her geometry, drawing a randomly placed array of circles, triangles and squares all over his body.

We all stood back, admiring our work. The room was dark, save for the TV switched to no particular channel – the haunting effervescence of the static filled screen making the room glow like an electric mist. I began to laugh.

"Wake up, Ciaran! Ciaran – Time to go!"

Ciaran jumped up with a drunken start.

"Time to go," he half mumbled, as he struggled to find his balance.

Alas, he could not find it. What he did find, however, was a gallop. We open the door, and allow him to gallop through it. The drunkest man I've ever seen, doing the drunkest run I've ever seen, painted as a gay, topless, geometric pirate, is now out wandering through the streets of Dublin at 3.00 a.m. just as the pubs and clubs are throwing out the last few drunken assholes – all looking for a fight because of the frustration that the night had ended before they did.

We returned to our casual drinking, and fell asleep at about five o'clock that morning.

It has been a tough week for my system. Rag week has just ended in college. I had started out on Monday morning as a newly built castle. Now, on Saturday night/Sunday morning, I am a nondescript ruin – the type archaeologists use their shovels to bury rather than examine.

I do not sleep well. I have fallen asleep on the bed of a friend of mine. He is already sleeping, and unaware of my presence. However, I rectify that by dreaming that he is on fire and waking myself up to try to beat out the flames. At 8.00 a.m., I realise that any attempt at sleep is futile. Time to face the day.

There is no point in bidding any of the sleeping 'farewells', so I put on my shoes and haul my internally mangled body out into the Sunday morning air. Trees wilt as I walk beneath them. Birds fall from the sky, dead, as they fly above me.

I have two pressing problems. First, I am hungry – very, very hungry. I have no money, however, and am at least an hour and a half from home, and from my mother's frying pan. It is Sunday – crap bus times – there'd be no direct bus until 10.00 a.m. I have to take a bus and walk for too many minutes from Lucan village.

My second problem is potentially a bigger one. I met an American girl earlier that week in college, and had arranged to meet her at 4.00 p.m. to go to a movie. If I had no money for food, I certainly had no money for entertaining. Anyway – she is just here for a week, and this isn't a date, is it? The thought does not last. I am unable to figure out which of my two problems is bigger. My stomach takes over. It is still drunk, and begins to give renditions of what sound like Tom Waits numbers. I need to stuff it with something – and fast. Within ten minutes, my stomach begins digesting itself, seeking sustenance for its singsong. What in God's name will I do?

As the answer to my problems appears before me, the Sunday morning church-bells ring out. Ah, Sunday. There, in front of me, on the footpath around Stephens Green, lies a small red and white box – open – with the words 'Southern Fried Chicken' printed on the side. In the box are two half-uneaten chicken legs – probably discarded by some drunken finger-licker during the previous night's revelries. (Ciaran, perhaps?) I stop, and bend down to get a closer look. My eyes confirm what my mind has perceived. There, in the box, lies the answer – the solution.

I pick up the box and look inside. My stomach grumbles hungrily as I pick up the half-eaten animal remnants between thumb and tip of index finger. I throw them aside, for it is what lies beneath them that I seek – a £10 note. Now, I can buy breakfast and have enough to buy popcorn for an American at the movies.

***

It's four o'clock and I am back in town. I have showered, put on fresh underwear (red and black jockey shorts, of all things!), and am wearing fume-free clothing. I am standing at Eason's, waiting for Nikki to arrive – looking right and left. She has black hair. I am looking for a black-haired head walking towards me. I do not see one. Ten minutes later and there is still no sign of an approaching head.

"Seán?" comes a tiny female voice.

I look around. I do not see anyone. 'Ah feck,' I think. 'That's all I need. A hangover that causes me to hear voices.'

"Hi, Seán," comes the voice a second time.

I look down. Down, a lot closer to the ground than my lowly head, is the black hair of an American. She is tiny. Much tinier than I remember from Wednesday night when I met her and her friends (a touring American Football team – all male, all huge) sitting on a bench in the Students Union pub in Maynooth University, my Alma Mater.

"Hi, Nikki," I say, hoping that she is too far away to see the confused look on my face. "Let's go to the movie."

I proceed to make some useless observation about the words 'movie' and 'talkie', and off we go. This crap comment is probably the most intelligent thing I will say all evening for, you see, I am a dud. I sleep through the movie. I am boring. I am uninteresting. I offer to take the bus back with her as far as Maynooth, where she is staying – seems like the decent thing to do.

Then, *it* happens. I had long been warned against giving my telephone number or home address to Americans. 'If you do that, they'll try to move in with you,' I was told. I heard horror stories about people who had done so when on holiday in the US – only to have the American arrive to Ireland on the next plane – the classic unexpected phone call from Dublin Airport of 'Hi – remember me? I pumped gas for you in Idaho on 26 November – I've come to visit for three weeks. Will you make up a bed for me and my family of eleven kids? Gee, thanks.'

Quite frankly, I do not believe these horror stories. Take Nikki, for example. Here is a normal enough twenty-something-year-old American travelling student looking to connect with people on a friendship level… or so I think.

You see, there is nothing between Nikki and me. I really think that we are just meeting as friends, and she gives me no clue that she is thinking any differently. Not until we are on the bus to Maynooth, that is.

"So, how will we do this?" she asks.

"Er, how will we do what?"

"How will we manage *us*?"

"Sorry?"

"Well, I finish College at the end of this semester. It will be at least three months until I can come back."

"What?"

"Or you could come to America – you could apply for a green card."

"A green card?"

"Wherever we end up, we should probably decide early on whether to rent a place or buy a place – my parents have money, so they could lend us the deposit on a house."

I am stunned into silence. What is she talking about? Why does she think that I am her missing half? Why...where...how do I figure out what the hell has just happened?

I mumble something about staying in touch, but not making any decisions until we are finished college. It isn't that I am trying to avoid the issue – I am trying to figure out what the issue is and how it has come about.

The following Thursday, she flies home. We have not seen each other since the bus-ride home. I get a letter from her a few weeks later, but never reply. This is my first real experience with America. I don't think about her much – but I imagine that she's become a lonely singer-songwriter, drifting through the American South singing songs about her lost love. Either that, or she married the taxi driver who took her to the airport – his offer to help her with her bags mistaken for a proposal of life-commitment.

***

I decide to study Anthropology in College as it is the only subject I know anything about. I opt to take a seminar called 'Out of the Bog and into the Culture' – a look at the role of bogs in Irish heritage as an elective in my Anthropology undergraduate. It is to be held each Wednesday in one of the older parts of Maynooth University, accessible via the Cardinal Newman footbridge ('Newman's Erection' to the students).

I take my seat in the dilapidated, uninspiring room with about five minutes to spare before the first class of the seminar begins. I take out a pen and foolscap pad, and begin to write in my unintelligible chicken scrawl as the lecturer talks.

About ten minutes into the class, the door opens. In walks an American – I can tell from her outrageously normal clothing. She sits a couple of chairs away from me. 'Cute,' I think.

The following Wednesday, she is there again, and still looking cute. 'I have talk to her,' I think. So I do. I ask her if she is going to the concert in the Student's Union bar that night. She is. I'll see her there. I go to a friend's house for an evening of wine and guitar beforehand.

"I think I have a date tonight."

"Really? With who?"

"An American girl from my Bog course."

"What's her name?"

"Feck. I can't remember."

Being unable to remember names is a talent that I have worked hard over the years to hone. No matter, though – I have a plan. I talk my friends into coming with me. I tell them to introduce themselves to her, thus forcing her to introduce herself to them. All I have to do is to be in earshot. It is foolproof. The doors open at about 8 o'clock. No need to be there until about 8.30 p.m.

At nine, I arrive outside the Students Union bar. I can't believe my eyes. Aslan have brought out the biggest crowd in Maynooth history. There are three times as many people as there are tickets. I am at the back of the queue.

I do what I have to do. I cut the queue. A friend near the top of the line lets me stand with her once I explain my dilemma. As it turns out, I am the last person they let in that night. My friend never makes it in. Nor do the friends who are going to help me with the name ruse. The American, however, is already inside.

I find her. She is with friends – her new flatmates. One of them saves my life.

"Marie – aren't you going to introduce us?"

Marie.

I introduce myself. Marie would later tell me that she had forgotten my name too, and also wasn't sure if this was a date or not. The night ends…well.

Soon, we are seeing more and more of each other. As a result of this, I start hanging out with the other Americans on campus and hearing their points of view on things. It is both an eye-opener and a reaffirmation of some previously-held stereotypes. It is also a lot of fun. I think I'm ready to go see the place. Marie leaves at the end of term. I arrange to follow.

***

My Dad drops me to the airport. I make my way straight to the Check-in desk and, from there, to the US Immigration desk in Dublin Airport. I take a Visa Waiver application form and begin to read it. The Visa Waiver form is designed to vet tourists before entering the country, to ensure that they will not pose a threat to the USA. I find the questions quite incredible. They are a series of Yes/No-type questions:

> *Do you have a communicable disease, physical or mental disorder, or are you a drug abuser or addict?*
> I answer 'No'.

> *Have you ever been or are you now involved in espionage or sabotage; or in terrorist activities; or genocide; or between 1933 and 1945 were you involved in any way in persecutions associated with Nazi Germany or its allies?*
> I can't recall any such activities, and again answer 'No'.

> *Have you ever been arrested or convicted for an offence or crime involving moral turpitude or a violation related to a controlled substance; or have been arrested or convicted for two or more offences for which the aggregate sentence to confinement was five years or more; or have been a controlled substance trafficker; or are you seeking entry to engage in criminal or immoral activities?*
> Tough one, this one.

Once completed, I join the line to hand the application form to an Immigration official. As I stand there, I look over the form and come to the conclusion that it is, in fact, an idiot test. Anyone that answers 'Yes' should rightly be denied a visa.

I look up and see that I am being called by an Immigration official – a woman of gargantuan proportions, including gargantuan orange hair styled in a gargantuan perm.

I do not recall the questions she asks me. In fact, the only thing I do recall is a feeling – one of pure intimidation. Her genuinely frightening demeanour delivers only one message: *Don't mess with Texas. Or wherever the hell it is you're going.*

My passport is stamped, and I am on my way – genuinely shaken, genuinely wary.

This is the first time I allow myself to truly be excited about the trip. There was always a niggling doubt that I would be the one they'd deny entry to. I call Marie and tell her to expect me in later that day. She cries – with what I hope is happiness.

I make my way to the Departure lounge. All around me are young Americans on their way home to the farm, having come abroad with their elasticated jeans to sample the Guinness and the men who drink it. I also see the young Irish – lads about my own age with wispy, bedraggled goatees made up of lonely beard spines all pointing in different directions. They look about 24 hours away from collecting glasses in Irish bars.

I think on it for a while, and realise something. Travel has become our rite of passage. We do not have initiation rites any more. We are not dragged off in the middle of the night by the village elders who stick feathers in our rectums and beat us with turnips. Or at least not any more. Thus, we have nothing that really marks our transition into adulthood. Except for travel. When we travel, we do so without our family. We take ourselves out of our comfort zones and deal with new challenges every day. We get to be adults – taking our own decisions, making our own mistakes and paying our own way. It is a boot-camp of sorts.

And why America? Simple. Because that's where the Irish have always gone. During famines, during recessions, during hard times – we went to America. When we had money and wanted a good time, we went to America. We go to America now because it has entered Irish folk mythology – simply – as the place we go.

I come back around to reality as the Tannoy announces boarding. I am on my way to America.

CHAPTER TWO

First Time in America

I manage to get a window seat on the plane. I am to fly to Newark and will change there for Minneapolis. I am wrong, however, to think that I might meet any Americans on the journey. The seat next to me is occupied by an Irishman, on his way to Toronto to relive the summer he spent there as a twenty-year-old some fifteen years previous. To make matters worse, not only is he travelling alone, but he has no one to visit in Toronto – all of the people he had met there have moved on.

Now, all of this would have been fine from my perspective if it was the kind of thing he slipped into casual conversation – you know the type – 'Hi. On your way to the US? Oh, I'm going to Toronto' – and then returning to his magazine or his in-flight movie.

But no. The root of his problem lies in the fact that he is a chain smoker. A fact he decides to use as an icebreaker with me.

"I'm a chain smoker."

'Good for you,' I think. A little irrelevant, but fair enough.

"I have to go seven hours without a fag."

I look at him. He is turning red, and begins sweating.

"I don't know how I'm going to go seven hours without a fag."

Incidentally, by this stage, the plane hasn't even fully boarded. We are still on the tarmac. We haven't even buckled our seat belts. I suspect that this is going to be a long, long journey.

After what seems a lifetime, the plane takes off. I am finally on my way west. I feel a little sense of adventure – kind of how Columbus or St Brendan would have felt I'm sure, if they were in a plane heading for the States. My sense of excitement is short-lived.

"Did – did I mention that I'm a chain smoker?"

Reaching up, he presses the call button above his head to get the attention of the stewardess. She comes, and he asks for a beer.

"Maybe this will quell the craving."

He is, by now, physically shaking. Ten minutes later, he has pressed the call button again, and is sparking open his second can. By the *tenth* can, the stewardesses are becoming worried – as am I. They face a dilemma. They can cut off his supply, and face an irate Irish drunk, or keep plying him with alcohol and hope that he'd remain sedate. Whatever the choice, it would be a bad one for me. They choose to keep the supply flowing. By the time the announcement comes that we are a mere 30 minutes from touching down in Newark, he orders his fourteenth can – I kid you not.

During the course of the journey, things get pretty surreal. The flight from Dublin to New York usually goes over the southern tip of Greenland. I am aware of this. So is he. Looking out the window, and leaning his sweaty, fume emitting body over me to do so, he sees what look to me to be clouds. But no – I am wrong apparently. They are icebergs, and the plane is flying too close to them. If we strike one, we'll go down.

I attempt to correct him. I shouldn't have. He is now more determined than ever. He now realises that we are flying too low, and that the pilots have not informed us, as they are too scared. That, or the pilots are dead and the plane is on autopilot. I look out the window. They still look pretty much like clouds to me.

"Maybe I should call the stewardess – tell her we're flying too low."

Reaching up again, he presses the call button. The stewardess duly arrives. He mumbles something about icebergs, and awaits her response. The young stewardess impresses me greatly.

"How about we get you another beer?"

There is a pause.

"Another beer would be nice."

He follows me off the plane in Newark. I give him the slip as we are making our way to the baggage reclaim. I don't know what became of him or his Toronto journey. He probably tried to look me up when he got back to Ireland, but had a problem trying to find a 'Charlie Doyle' listed in the Wicklow phone book.

***

I am in. I am the first member of my immediate family to make it to America. I feel a weird sense of pride.

I walk down a long, tall, white corridor that connects the landing gates with the rest of the airport. I turn around a corner and behold what is for me an awesome sight. At the end of the corridor stands a massive white Portland stone arch. 'Welcome to the United States of America' it states silently as we file beneath it. For a moment, I know how the provincials must have felt when entering Rome for the first time two millennia ago. The arch is majestic, simple, powerful, daunting and beautiful. An arch is psychologically more powerful than a sign – the mere act of passing through it suggests 'dominance' – a rebirth that it controls. I am in.

Newark airport looks a model of efficiency. It is clean and functional. I would later learn that it was designed on the same principals as almost every other airport in North America, and there really is nothing special about it. It will be my home for the next three hours, as I wait for my connection to Minneapolis. 'An excellent chance for some people-watching,' I think.

I make my way to the departure gate with surprising ease. Coming from Dublin airport, which, because of IRA activity, has a visible security presence, I find the airport security here to be downright incompetent. At the entrance to the departure area there are the usual mini-arches that screen the passengers for metallic objects. I pass through – electric guitar in hand. There is, however, no one manning the station. I somewhat cautiously continue on. In Dublin, I am used to showing my boarding pass at this stage – no non-passengers allowed into the Departure area. That is not the case here. There are entire families walking one family member *all the way to the boarding gate!* There are obvious pickpockets able to enter and leave the departure area at will. It is all very unsettling. It will be proven that my unsettled feeling was not without reason for, you see, I enter the USA on 11 September 2000 – a year to the day before the attack.

My gate is all the way down the end of the departure area. An announcer's voice comes on the intercom system:

"Could Mr Buttoni please pick up the nearest courtesy telephone and contact Japotti."

I am beginning to experience what I studied as part of my Anthropology undergraduate – culture shock. The names are different – Buttoni and Japotti. The clothes are different. I experience something that my brother will experience in Tunisia two years later. He will tell me that he wasn't sure how to file away his experience in Tunis – he didn't know if the people were nice or not because he can't tell, as he put it, who the scumbags are. I am having the same problem. A young guy – about twenty years old – Chinese by origin, possibly, is wearing what I only know to be gang clothes. Is he merely trendy or trying to decide if the triads should declare war on the bearded Irishman now on their territory? For my entire layover in Newark, he paces up and down past my gate, making me feel very nervous – he doesn't have any luggage, and doesn't seem to be travelling anywhere.

The announcer comes back over the intercom:

"Would Passenger Smith travelling to Salt Lake City please contact Japotti."

Interesting – there's another guy called Japotti. 'Must be a common local surname,' I think.

Finally, I find my gate. As there is another two hours to boarding, I am one of the only people waiting. I sit myself down, facing the corridor, so that I can make more of my ethnographical observations. No sooner have I sat down than a big, big fat man walks by. I have never seen such a young man so obese before. He is poorly dressed too – baggy blue jeans and a faded blue denim shirtsleeves rolled up. The shirt is not tucked in. I reckon that this is more out of necessity that fashion – he has really, really fat arms. They are almost perched upon his belly, making it look like he is constantly trying to grab something – food, no doubt. Possession of such arms, I figure, would make the act of shirt-tucking a pipe dream – now no more reachable than being an astronaut or an Olympic ice skater. It is to get worse.

Suddenly, the announcer is back on air.

"Would Mr and Mrs Buvomatizie travelling to St Louis please contact Japotti."

'OK,' I think. 'This is getting strange. Who is Japotti? I have to put my thinking cap on, just in case I needed to deal with him/her.'

There is, however, to be little time for such ponderings. No sooner has the obese man struggled from my sight, when a woman who gives the appearance of having dined exclusively on obese men walks slowly over to a Cinnabon stand, resting her girth on the counter. She is huge – and, again, poorly dressed in faded black denim jeans. They are ill-fitting – it almost looks as if she has stuffed two arse cheeks down one leg.

The Cinnabon assistant approaches her. He is almost as big as she is. I slowly began to look around. I notice that around two out of every three people are massive. In all my life, I have never seen so much fat. It is repulsive, but it is endlessly fascinating. I take out one of my travel guides to see if any of these lardopod landmarks are shown on any maps. They are not.

"Would Mrs Harris, travelling to Bangor, Maine, please contact Japotti."

I noticed that in most cases, these obese people are poorly dressed. Their clothes seem to either be too small or an afterthought. It is not until about three months later when I remark to an American acquaintance (who I have assumed is comfortable in her bulk) that she is a little overweight that I realise what is going on. The acquaintance immediately becomes defensive and lectures me on ideals of normal weight, etc., etc. That is when I would realise that the obese in America appear to be so poorly dressed because they dress as how they would like to be – not as they are.

Suddenly, another announcement comes over the intercom. It is, however, a different voice – not the rough-hewn female Japotti-lover that I come to love.

"Would Mr Chang travelling to Anchorage please contact your party."

The mystery is over. I wondered how the New York accent told of other parties. For example, does 'I spent hours at the party' become 'I spent hours at the potty'? The song 'It's my party and I'll cry if I want to' now has a completely different meaning for me. I also now suspect that I probably would cry too if it happened to me.

There is something else I notice that feels alien to me. When I was a teenager, I worked weekends and holidays in a particularly quiet Burger King in Dublin. I had a really great time working there, and met lots of interesting characters. One Chinese guy I worked with – who, incidentally, went by the name Seán – told me that he couldn't believe how friendly and apologetic everyone in Dublin is to each other. If you bumped into someone, the chances are that the bumpee would apologise to the bumper. He and his friends actually used to go out onto the busier streets to bump into people and get an apology. They thought it the funniest thing ever. In Newark, I notice the opposite. Like everywhere, I see some people bumping into others. But they are being shouted at for doing so. It is all so different.

Finally, the call comes to board the flight to Minneapolis. I make my way down the gangway and board the 737 for the last leg of my journey. This time, I am sitting in the emergency aisle, about half way down the aircraft. I've always preferred this as the legroom is better and the proximity of the emergency exit could prove useful. Sitting beside me in the window seat is a man dressed suspiciously like a commercial pilot.

'Damn back seat driver,' I think.

Soon, we are talking. He is indeed a pilot – but is not in charge of this particular craft, I am relieved to hear. Apparently, he gets free travel as long as he is in uniform. He is a genuinely likable man – late forties, carrying a little weight.

"On your way to see family?" I enquire.

"No – on my way to see my girlfriend. It's been almost a month since I've seen her."

"Must be hard for you," I comment. He smiles.

Turns out that it isn't as hard as one might expect. For, you see, the 'girlfriend' in question is just the girlfriend at this particular port. He had spent the previous weekend with a fiancée in Atlanta and the weekend before with a girlfriend in Denver.

"One of the perks of the job."

I am afraid to tell him that I am on my way to live with my girlfriend for a few months – I am still pretty shaken from the Immigration ordeal, and want as few people as possible to know about my existence in America. I tell him that I am staying with a friend that night, lest he fix me up with a spare girlfriend.

"Why Minnesota, anyway?"

"I just fancied coming somewhere where I am more or less guaranteed to get away from it all – somewhere where I won't bump into any Irish, or meet anyone who knows my father. That's why I chose Minnesota over New York or Chicago."

With that – I swear – the guy in the seat behind me taps me on the shoulder.

"Howya – I'm from Blackrock." A feckin' Dub.

The plane lands just after 6.00 p.m. into Minneapolis-St Paul airport. The previous three hours has taken me over some beautiful scenery, including Lake Michigan and what seemed to be a thousand tiny Minnesotan lakes. The plane swoops down over the dark and foreboding Mississippi before landing. Not bad going – only six hours here and I already reached the centre of the continent.

I bid farewell to my testosterone-driven friend, and head for the Arrivals hall. I turn a corner. There stands Marie. We hug and, until the hug is over, do not let go.

We hail a taxi at the rank beneath the airport. It is evening by now. I am tired because of the trip, but also excited, for in just a few moments I get my first proper look at one of the great American cities, Minneapolis.

Minneapolis and St Paul are collectively known as the Twin Cities due to the fact that they are so close to each other. They have definable city centres of their own, but the surrounding areas have meshed into a large suburbia – one without definition.

The taxi pulls out of the Lindbergh Terminal of the airport – named for the famous Minnesotan aviator. (I suspect they've forgotten about his Nazi sympathies). Soon, we are speeding down Highway 55, past Fort Snelling, the oldest building in the state despite dating back only as far as the 1820s.

Everything looks…different. For a start, the cars are different – all huge and run-down. It seemed that quantity, not quality, counted when it comes to automobile girth. Even the taxi-cab has a rim of rust running along its flanks. The buildings look different. The streets look different.

There is one difference above all that captures my imagination. The sky. I can't believe how high up it is. It is not something I expected – but it is still the first thing I notice whenever I go back. Coming from Ireland, I'm used to the visible sky being quite low. On particularly grey days being outdoors can almost feel like being indoors – the clouds become like a roof.

In America – or at least in Minnesota – the clouds are much farther away. Ireland seems to have an extra layer of cloud just above building level that boxes us all in. In America, that layer does not exist. The sky is everywhere. It gives a great sense of freedom and of possibility. Only in recent years have I discovered something similar in Dublin – looking up to the top of Dublin's Spire, one suddenly realises that the sky is part of the city too.

***

Marie is anxious for me to meet the people that make up her world.

I had already met her mother when she visited Marie in Ireland the previous March. I remember trying to focus on being polite, and ended up coming across as boring and uninteresting. I'll be careful not to make that mistake again.

And indeed I don't make that mistake again. I am not boring or uninteresting. But I am still a total disaster. I am due to meet Marie's sister on the evening that I arrive. But I have a problem – one I have not experienced before, but which has become all too familiar since. It is a curse that was only discovered in the 20th century, one that has plagued Man ever since: jet lag.

The Lag hits me straight away. It is horrible. It is loud. It is deafening. It hits in waves. It is relentless. I have since learned that keeping hydrated more or less prevents it, and that sleeping is not necessarily the best thing for it. But back then, I didn't know what to do.

The first time I ever got drunk – really, really drunk – happened at a house party that a friend threw when his family were away on holidays. I was eighteen, and two days away from finishing my Leaving Cert – the last big exams before University. I only had my first drink a few months earlier. There were still many drinking frontiers to cross and barriers to break. That night, we started off in the pub. I drank Tia Maria. I had four doubles, neat, on ice. Back to the house. I had an entire mug of vodka – no ice, no mixer. I was pallatic (paralytic). I could not stand up. At about 1.00 a.m., some more people arrived at the party. They brought a bottle of golden Tequila. I snatched it from them, opened it up and put it to my lips. I consumed (according to witnesses) about a quarter of the bottle in one go.

I have never – in all of my life – been as drunk since. I walked home. It is usually a four-minute walk, but it would take me close to an hour. I would wake up the next morning, my head in a pool of vomit on my pillow. A streak of vomit had sprayed the walls. I was sick – and deserved every throb of it.

It is my first – and worst – hangover. It is three days before I can eat properly again. It is a month before I can take a drink again. I feel like my body has died, but has forgotten to tell my brain. Even though I have since learned my lesson and rarely drink at all, the memory of the humiliation persists.

The jet lag feels like a cross between the drunkenness and the hangover. It is awful. I don't know what to do. My brain goes from being fully aware and in search of stimulation to completely shut-down and in search of a place to sleep all within the space of a second or two. It lasts for days – but peaks on the first evening. Everything looks like a cosy bed to me – car seats, bus stops, sidewalks. The people I meet over the next few days would not be judged by my usual criteria – instead, I think about how rested they look. I want to ask them how they sleep. I am curious as to whether or not they'd have any objection to me fluffing them up like a pillow and climbing on for a nap.

Over we go to Marie's sister's apartment. It is nice – very nice for a student apartment. My over-riding memory is of the mosaic of smashed mirror tiles on the living room wall.

"This is Seán," says Marie.

I wake up and introduce myself. Then I begin a very peculiar conversation – one that has haunted me ever since. This is because I still haven't got the slightest notion about what I was trying to say.

First, I started talking about jet lag – about how the lag is attacking me in waves. That starts a conversation about travel. Fair enough – seems appropriate. Then, I think that it would be a great opportunity to talk about phrenology – the 'science' of intellect and head size. Why? I don't know. But – to make matters worse, I can't remember the word 'phrenology'. I scan my brain looking for it. What I find is not 'phrenology'. In fact, what I find is not even remotely related to it. The word that my brain gave me to use in this already surreal conversation is…dendrochronology. The study of tree rings. I prattle on for about nine or ten minutes on the subject – much to the bemusement of Marie and her sister. My brain is so tired it is hurting. Soon, Marie makes our excuses, and we leave – no doubt in a hurry in case I might add to this already fantastic first impression. When I later asked her sister about it, she told me something that would make me cringe:

"Don't worry – I know you had jet lag."

***

My earliest casual encounters with America came through the medium of TV. I still have five or six vivid memories of the first house I lived in. Although we moved from it when I was only four years old, I can remember my father returning from playing football one day; a mouse running up the curtains; the dog, Shelly, playing in the garden; and seeing *Dallas* and *The A-Team* on TV. *Dallas* and *The A-Team* are particularly interesting, as between the two of them, they personify much of American culture – wealth, oil, sex and guns. Throw in the inevitable McDonalds' commercials between the shows and you've got a virtual guide to America in fifty-five minutes.

Almost all of us have been exposed to American culture and its value systems through TV. We learn about family life through *The Brady Bunch*. We learn about justice through *The A-Team* and *Ally McBeal*. We learn about food through McDonalds ads. We learn about the lives we should aspire to through *Dallas*. What we don't learn are real life-skills. We feel frustrated when we don't resolve our problems in a half-hour like they do on TV. We learn that McDonalds food must be good for us – after all, it's recommended to us on TV by a smiling clown.

My own first direct experience with TV in America comes shortly after my arrival there – the first morning, in fact. I switch on the TV – a rather old, cable-less affair, and tune in a local Minneapolis station. There is an ad for a car windshield repair company. The ad consists of three mechanics running around the place in a series of ill-conceived sporting events. I soon gather that this is a reference to the Olympics that is taking place on TVs across the US each night. The men in the ad prattle on about their low prices for a while. Then comes the tag line: 'Order now, and receive a free box of steak'. What, I wonder, could that mean? What is the word 'steak' a reference to? Perhaps a brand of windscreen cleaner? Who knows? That evening, I ask my girlfriend soon after she arrives in from work. Apparently, 'steak' means 'steak'. The windshield company in question has become famous for it: free steak with every windscreen purchased. Here in a thirty second nutshell is American culture. Sales. Low prices. Sports. Cars. Meat.

I am a long, long way from home.

I risk sounding pompous here when I talk about American TV. I should point out that I eventually decided that it is simply different to what we have, and that a citizen of a country that can get hooked so easily on reality TV shows and find-a-star programmes is in no position to criticise.

***

About a week into my stay, I decide to go downtown to have a proper look around. Marie is working, so I have the day to myself. I take out a city map, and memorise the way – I plan to walk. It takes me about forty minutes to walk from Dinkytown to Hennepin Avenue. I walk over a Mississippi bridge and pause briefly to spit into the mighty river below. I've made a point to spit into every major body of water that I encounter in the world, to satisfy the neurotic in me.

I find walking a little unsettling – mainly because I am the *only* one doing so. I would later learn that there are only very specific areas of the city in which people walk – but then it's only for recreation and exercise. Nobody walks to get places. I feel, and must have looked, out of place. Actually – that's not entirely true. In my journal, I make the following entry:

'I feel…not so much out of place myself as everything here seems to be.'

Soon, I am almost at Hennepin – the city centre proper. I don't know what to expect. I am now walking among the buildings that comprise the skyline – the usual collection of tall skyscrapers that, from a distance, give the impression of wealth, opulence and sophistication. These are three adjectives that I would not encounter on this day.

There is a scene in the movie *Trading Places* where Eddie Murphy is a bum masquerading as a Vietnam veteran. He is pretending that he has no legs and is scooting along in a cart. It is people like this that I see in downtown Minneapolis. The first man I encounter is a black man, wearing a red and blue bandana and a green vest. He has long since replaced his teeth with gums. He is asking people for change. And by the way – he is hauling himself around in a cart. Looking around, these are the only people I see *at all*. They are looking at me – and they are smiling. I have, however, no change to give them.

It is all very unsettling. It seems to me to be the worst poverty I have ever seen. I'm not sure if this is because of the contrasting setting, or the actual poverty level itself – but it is shocking nonetheless. It is not to be the only such shock during my stay.

As I venture further into the centre, to the entrances to the skyscrapers, the homeless disappear. All I see now are office workers. For, you see, in downtown Minneapolis, there is not much to do unless you either work in an office or want to beg from office workers. There's not much in the way of shops or restaurants. They are there, but not in abundance. This side of the city's life has dwindled since the opening of the Mall of America – the biggest shopping mall in the world – in the Minneapolis suburb of Bloomington.

I feel more like a stranger in this city than I have in any other I've ever visited. I even feel more out of place here than I did in Frankfurt, Germany, where a guy stopped me once on the underground and asked if the female friend I was out with was 'for sale'. All afternoon, I tried to figure out what it is about the city that I don't feel comfortable with.

Then it comes to me. It is the history – or, to be more precise, the lack thereof. Dublin, for example, is made up of several layers. There is a medieval layer of the city around Christchurch Cathedral. There is the Georgian layer around Merrion Square. There is the Victorian layer around the south suburbs. There is the Irish Free State layer – which consists of new buildings at select locations in the city centre. There is the Irish Republic layer, which consists of the same, and several drab suburbs.

It all comes together to form 'Dublin'. It means that Dublin isn't merely one city, but a collection of cities that have built up over time. The people are like this too – all with their own experiences and interpretations of Dublin and of community. If you don't like the Dublin you are living in, you can move to another while retaining the same address.

In Minneapolis, it seemed different. There is only one city layer – and it is only about a hundred years only. The suburbs all look the same (all eerily like Malmö in Sweden, incidentally). There is a feeling that Minneapolis is only one city, and that you have to either like it or lump it. The locals haven't been there really long enough to establish other Minneapolises yet, which is perhaps why there's such a great boom in psychological problems in America. The country isn't old enough in many cases to provide the people with an alternative. Thus, when someone has a problem, they try to fix it so that they can fit in – they have no place else to go.

***

Shopping is an interesting experience in America – particularly food shopping. I had been told by Irish who have visited America that the food is very inexpensive. I therefore have not budgeted much money for it.

On my first night in America, we go to Target – a large national chain that sells *everything*. I make straight for the local candy section, being somewhat of a connoisseur myself. I am overwhelmed by choice. I buy several things to try – including Tootsie Rolls, Candy Corn, Whoppers and Hershey's chocolate.

When we have finished in Target, having also purchased underwear, we go next door to a Supermarket, where I want to do some food shopping. I've always fancied myself as a bit of a cook. I prefer to cook food rather than assemble it. I know that it's pompous, but I consider ready-made sauce mixes etc. as cheating.

I take a trolley – sorry, 'shopping cart' – from the bay, and enter the store. I go to the Fruit & Veg section. I am appalled; everything is so very, very expensive. Perplexed, I ask Marie if she knows why everything is so expensive – I understood the opposite to be true. And, it turns out, the opposite *is* true – so long as you don't buy fresh, unprocessed foods with the intention of actually cooking. In fact, I swear that the shopping cart had to be guided through the Fruit & Veg section with extra determination – it had never been in that section before! We throw a few ears of corn in the cart and continue on.

When in Rome…We end up buying things that I have heard of on TV, but have never tried. I have never had waffles, for example, so we buy frozen, pre-packed waffles. The same goes for Chilli and Burritos. We also buy Oreos.

I find a magazine stand close to the checkouts. It is filled with the usual assortment of Ricki Lake-type journals. It also sells little books – puzzle books, cookbooks etc. I pick one of the more popular cookbooks to have a quick browse. I can't believe what is passing for a recipe. The first I encounter is a recipe called 'Chicken in a Mushroom Sauce'.

'Oh good,' I think. 'I've never been able to get my mushroom sauce completely right. Maybe this will help me.'

Nope.

Ingredients:
Chicken fillets.
Can of mushroom soup.

Method:
Pour contents of can over chicken. Bake.

The next recipe is for Italian Tomato Chicken.

Ingredients:
Chicken fillets.
Can of Italian Tomato soup.

I am horrified. That isn't cooking. I show it to Marie, expecting to get a laugh from her at the absurdity of it all. Nope. It is normal, she tells me. Sure enough, a particularly well-known canned soup manufacturer – let's call them 'Canbells' – no – too obvious – we'll call them 'Kambells' – actually advertises the recipes on thirty second TV slots. I've even found these recipes in the healthy eating recipe of the week section of 'good living' magazines! This all seems so foreign to me.

We get home and throw on our frozen, ready-to-eat waffles. When ready, we open up a can of processed, ready-to-eat cherries and a can of cream – just like you'd find in Nature. We put it all together, and tuck in. We are joined by friends, curious to see the Irelander. The others around the table are moaning and groaning – oh how good this is, etc. I am also moaning and groaning – but for very different reasons. After the first bite, I take my fork and run it carefully over the waffle. I am convinced from the taste that it is still in its original plastic. It does not seem to be. I check the cherries – perhaps the red fruity sauce they are in is actually a form of mould. It is not. I pick up the squirty cream and check the date, thinking that maybe by accident the company had sent out a batch of their original squirty cream from the 1950s, and it has now simply gone off. It has not. What is even more disturbing is that the sugar level in the cream would ensure that it would probably *never* go off.

Marie, sensing that all is not well, diplomatically suggests that I try another – this time with syrup. Syrup, eh? The kind they eat in the movies? If I eat it, I'll be just like a real movie star. Alright, I'll do it.

Another soggy and oddly slippery waffle is flopped down onto my plate. I am handed a plastic bottle of syrup. I look at the bottle to see what I would be eating. Is it maple syrup? Is it a honey-based syrup? Alas, not having a background in Experimental Chemistry means that I cannot decipher the ingredients. There is, however, a friendly looking black woman on the bottle. She is smiling at me – unlike the gun-wielding black man I have seen on the television that afternoon. Wanting to encourage this smiling behaviour, I decide to try her syrup. I pour a little onto my waffle.

"No – you need to smother it."

I think I understand – the waffle might still be alive. Better not take any chances, and drown it.

Soon, my waffle is glistening like a 1970s yellow smoked glass dinner set. Cautiously, I cut a slice, and remove a wedge. My teeth squelch into it. The flavours are released. It tastes like…the machinery it is made in.

"I'm sorry," I say. "I can't eat this."

I leave it at that – however, my mind continues, screaming at me '… because it tastes like ASS! What's wrong with you people? How can you eat this shite?'

I decide, however, that it would be impolite to share these musings with my hosts.

Following the evening's culinary curiosities, we retire to the sitting room, where the curiosities cease to be culinary, and become candied – the same purchased in Target. I unwrap a Tootsie Roll and pop it into my mouth. Next, I try some Candy Corn. Following this, a chunk of Hershey's chocolate.

The candy experience leads me to greater understanding of the USA. America, as we all know, is one of the most oil dependent nations on the planet. It uses this oil for a multitude of reasons: fuels; petrochemicals; getting rich. It also uses it in the production of the only other substance aside from oil with which America has become synonymous. Ancient Rome and Greece are synonymous with stone, for example, as are the great builders of Egypt. The Irish have, to a greater or lesser degree, become associated with the less permanent alcohol. And so on. America has become synonymous with plastic.

It is interesting to look at the culture of association in the world. In Greece and Rome, a polytheistic society based its beliefs on personifying the elementals of our world, and ended up using stone to build its temples and metals to adorn its leaders. In Ireland, the local pub is the main focus of socialising and business. The Guinness brewery in Dublin is a revered and hallowed site. St Patrick's Day is now a true Irish festival – a drinking binge that is the latest in a long line that includes St Kevin's

Day – a Victorian celebration that horrified all bar the Irish themselves. St Patrick's day is also the day on which we celebrate our national identity. Coincidence?

In America, every day is a potential celebration of national identity. America is so present in global affairs that it achieves something almost every day. Chants of 'USA! USA!' are not uncommon at sporting events. And, of course, this means that extra reverence is paid to the national symbols. Plastic is no exception. Not only is it passively worshipped – mock-plastic is eaten in the form of Tootsie Rolls, Candy Corn and, arguably the most appalling of all America's edible exports, Hershey's chocolate, which tastes only one wick short of eating a candle. Yes, that long ranting diatribe was for a short, cheap joke about American candy tasting like plastic. An Oreo experience, incidentally, is not like a plastic-chewing experience – although, I can assure you that this is more a reflection on their texture than their taste. Even the thought of it – a cookie produced by a multinational tobacco conglomerate – does nothing for me. Hmm – I wonder if they've considered this as a slogan?

I never had much – or any – experience of Mexican food. It is, however, very popular in America. Each state seems to have its own interpretation of what 'Mexican' is. In Minnesota, for example, it is not spicy. In Washington State, I will find the opposite.

My first experience with Mexican food comes on my first evening. Fighting horrible, wave-like jet lag, I venture out with Marie and a friend to Chipotle – a burrito chain. I order a beef burrito with all the fixin's. (Note – Minnesotans do not use the word 'fixin's' – I just like it). Basically, the tortilla wrap contains 'spiced' beef and a little greenery of some kind (probably that nutritionally superior and immensely tasty vegetable that America has rightfully made the world take note of – Iceberg Lettuce). There are also a few black beans and a little white rice. I estimate that these ingredients take up about one third of the capacity of the unleavened receptacle. The rest is filled with various…pastes. There is a cream cheese paste, a sour cream paste, a guacamole paste that tastes like it contains a little of every ingredient known to Man except for avocado, and a salsa. The salsa is particularly disappointing – it contains chunks of things (tomato, onion, etc.) but does not form any coherent flavour.

A cook is akin to a general. The cook selects the appropriate ingredients, prepares them carefully, and blends them until they are no longer individuals – they are now a small part of a new dish. The vegetables in the salsa are the result of a leaderless army – each having been mangled into bite-sized pieces well before its time. Each piece now stands alone, unaware that they are all supposed to be part of a salsa.

In I bite. I taste fat. Everyone likes a little butter on toast – or maybe a vegetable-based spread. This does not mean that everyone likes to sit down with a tub of 'I Can't Believe It's Not Butter' and a spoon, hoping to get to the bottom before they are asked to share. This principle does not seem to apply with food pastes in America.

'People like guacamole. Let's add lots of it. People like sour cream too. Let's add lots of this too. The more we add, the more they'll like it.'

Then economic efficiency kicks in.

'No – lets add lots of green paste and white paste instead – if it looks like guacamole and sour cream, no one will know the difference.'

In short, the burrito is nothing but a delivery device for chemically-enhanced fat.

I am particularly upset at this – Chipotle is the one food that I have been promised by many I would enjoy. I am, however, unable to get through more that three or four bites. I even give it a second chance – bringing it home and putting it in the fridge for breakfast. By morning, it has congealed – not a state that should be sought by cooks, no matter what the food in question. The funny thing is, when I arrive home a little over three months later, having never returned to Chipotle, it is these burritos that I crave above any other food.

***

At lunchtime next day, Marie suggests that we have the ears of corn that we have recently bought. Now, corn is something that I have encountered in Ireland. In fact, I counted it amongst the foods I favoured most. I would usually order it as a starter in Irish restaurants. It normally comes served smothered in melted butter. It is never an entire ear of corn – usually the middle piece. The tapered thirds attached to either end are either discarded or de-kerneled and canned. The corn I know is frozen. It is yellow. Yellower than that. The kernels are always a little shrivelled – but that is corn.

Conversations about corn were a mainstay of the early days of our relationship in Ireland. I tell her that I am a fan of corn. She is amazed. She doesn't think that Ireland has the climate to grow corn. A hint of horror creeps across her face as I confirm the fact that Ireland's climate is more suited to corn importation than corn production. A full-blown look of horror takes over her face as I go further, telling her of the condition in which it is imported – namely frozen.

"Frozen corn? You actually eat frozen corn?"

"Yep. I'll make some for you."

"I spent my summers in Michigan. How do you expect someone who grew up eating Michigan corn to eat frozen crap?"

"It's not 'crap'. I promise you, you'll enjoy it if you tried it."

Over to Superquinn we go. I remove a pack of frozen corn from the freezer section. The picture of the large green man on the front looks promising – would I grow to be as big and muscular if I ate this corn? Would I turn green? Who knew?

Back to my parents' house.

Pot of water on.

Boiling.

Frozen corn plonked inside.

Simmer.

Simmer.

Remove.

Butter substitute smeared on.

Corn holders inserted.

"Here you go, Marie."

I take my cob in hand and begin crunching.

"Mmmm."

I look at Marie. There is no *mmmm* or consonants of any kind coming from her. In fact, there is no noise – period. There has been one crunch – but it has not been followed by others. How very strange.

"Mmmm," I venture a second time.

"I can't eat this. I'm sorry."

"Why not? I think you said you liked corn."

"This is not 'corn'. This is crap. It's all…fleshy. The taste is awful. How can you eat this?"

"Because I like corn."

Flash forward eight months. Corn preparation in America doesn't seem that different – in principle – to corn preparation back home. The peeling of the husks seems similar to the opening of the packet. Corn is placed into water. The water is brought to the boil. The corn – an entire ear, lesser thirds included – is removed on boiling. After being removed from the water, 'butter-substitute substitute' (or butter, as it is also known) is rubbed into the corn. Sea salt, fresh black pepper.

"Corn's ready."

Marie takes the first crunch.

"It's not bad – I've had better," she says.

"As good as the frozen corn back in Ireland?"

"Just eat the corn."

My tongue doesn't know how to process the culinary sensations it has been presented with. Should it concentrate on the unsurpassable flavour of fresh American corn or on the bitter, sour taste of my words?

My first experience of fresh American corn is one of the culinary highlights of my life. It is sublime. I cook and eat another two ears that night. By morning, it is the my only faecal constituent. Every time I go back to the American Mid-West (at the right time of the year) I buy and eat some fresh, local corn. Eating it is now a ritual. No trip is complete without it – although I do get a little carried away.

Soaking the corn in water for an hour to bulk it up to its prime. Peeling it back to reveal the yellow colour of the kernels – pale and healthy. Boiling the lightly salted water. Simmering the corn. Rubbing the butter, adding the salt and pepper. Crunching. Eating. Getting carried away. Making another. And another. Eating a fourth. Suffering from a grumbly bowel. Looking at small, chewed kernels floating in the toilet bowl. Going to sleep with a hollow, diarrhoeic feeling. Getting up the next morning. Making corn for breakfast. I just can't seem to get enough. I've turned into Marie's corn ego. Since my first corn experience, I haven't touched frozen corn. I consider it to be crap. In my dreams, I am Marie, arguing with old Seán about the virtue of fresh corn.

***

I have been invited by Marie's mom to go to her house in Duluth for Thanksgiving. Unsure as to just why she wanted to thank me, I allow my curiosity to accept the invitation. Perhaps she had resigned herself to having an unmarriageable daughter and is grateful to me for dating her. *I really hope that Marie doesn't read this!*

Thanksgiving takes place on the last Thursday in November. We would be attending a Saturday rerun, so that more family could gather. As Marie has a week off, I manage to clear a few days from my busy schedule. A week in Duluth is in the offing. We plan to arrive in Duluth the Monday beforehand, giving us a good week to hang out. And better still – we planned to take the Greyhound.

Now, riding an actual greyhound from Minneapolis to Duluth is not only unethical, but illegal. This fact does not depend on the cities in question, but is a general nationwide principle. Even if it was legal, I doubt that it would be very practical. Instead, the Greyhound in question is an MC-12, 55-seater Greyhound bus. Not unlike an actual greyhound, it has a driver/brain at the front, a toilet function at the back, and an entrance where the ears would be   but, of course, this final analogy only works if humans are compared to ear parasites. Here, the similarities end – except for the wheels, which can actually be purchased for not only Greyhounds, but any canine in question that requires a back leg amputation – sort of like a wheelchair for dogs. But I digress.

I am excited about riding the Greyhound. It is, after all, an American cultural icon, as depicted in such Hollywood glamour pics as, er, *Midnight Cowboy*. We arrive at the Minneapolis Greyhound station about forty-five minutes before the bus is due to depart. How do I know this? My gigantic book of USA train and bus timetables, of course, which I bought for my trip. Although the Twin Cities to Duluth is a straightforward, three-hour journey, I spend two days planning it. The bus always stops in Hinckley, I am told, for a fifteen-minute break – about two hours outside of the Cities. Hinckley would later become, for me, one of the highlights of North America because of a certain bakery called 'Tobies'. I had been told quite a bit about it, and was relishing the prospect of a fifteen-minute gorge fest.

We purchase our tickets, and go to the waiting area. It is smaller than I had anticipated – especially for a large urban area like the Twin Cities. It is basically one large room with a snack bar and a magazine stand. To my delight, however, the magazine stand has…Greyhound souvenirs! Never one to even attempt resisting tacky crap, I go over to inspect their wares. My eyes, and budget, focus in on a Greyhound thimble. 'I better buy it before they sell out,' I think to myself. So I do.

Soon, the call comes, and we walk to our vessel. We sit in a double seat down the back. The driver arrives, and gives a nice little introductory speech, in which we are told that we can't drink, can't smoke and can't have sex on his bus. And we are off.

We drive through the twin cities – through Midtown. Past the Watchtower from the Bob Dylan song. Through Frogtown. Through Little France. I can honestly say that in all of my life, I never seen such poverty. These areas are little more than paved shantytowns – although the people living there seem happy enough. We drive past the State

Capitol in St Paul – the governor being former pro-wrestler Jesse Ventura. A couple more stops and we are out of the cities, and cruising along Route I-35. This is my first chance to see something else other than urban America.

I am…disappointed. All we see is the highway. The reason for this is that it is impossible to see past the advertising hoardings. They are everywhere. There are ads for Casinos. For Churches. For Contraception. For Abortion. For the Pro-Lifers. For Adoption. For More Casinos. For Fast Food. For advertising space. I have never seen anything like it.

The advertising plague is something I notice shortly after arriving in the USA. Ads are everywhere. Park benches, for example, far from being inviting and small idyllic oases of calm in an urban desert devoid of rest, they are advertising hoardings with legs. Ads are even in public restrooms – a phenomenon that has since caught on in Europe. Peeing on a urinal splashguard reveals the message. TV is all about ads – literally ads every five to ten minutes.

More than anything else, I find this fact hardest to come to terms with. The density of advertising in urban America serves as a distraction from everything. It is not possible to get lost in one's thoughts. Every nice piece of contemplative scenery is marred by an advertising hoarding. Every provocative half hour of quality TV drama is repeatedly interrupted by a plethora of pointless, poorly produced product placements. I even see the phrase 'Worshipping is not a spectator sport' written above the altar of a local church – slogan as the new scripture.

Soon, we begin to see ads for Tobies bakery in Hinckley. *Mmmm.* Tobies. I have never visited – but having gorged for a while on Tobies legends and stories, I know what to expect. Hinckley – 15 Miles. Hinckley – 10 Miles. Hinckley – Next Exit…

And we drive past it. We take the next exit. Soon, the bus comes to a standstill. The driver informs us that we have fifteen minutes to stretch our legs. Great, I think. But where in the hell are we?

Every town has something for which it is known. New York is known for the Statue of Liberty. Hinckley is known for Tobies. We are in

Sandstone, which is known for its massive Federal penitentiary. Nice.

We stop at a gas station just down the road from it. Great. Poor, pre-packaged plastic again. I take $10 and buy Tootsie Rolls and Candy Corn.

Soon, we are on our way. Tobies would have to wait – both me for it, and it for me. We have brought water with us. By the time we reach Sandstone, we have consumed about a litre between us. I have to pee. I can't find the bathroom in Sandstone – not that I actually needed a bath, mind you. That leaves me with one option. Peeing on the bus.

I enter the mobile bathroom at the back of the bus. There, I behold a very odd sight. First of all, the toilet is not free standing – it is more a hole in a shelf. I also noticed that there is no handle to flush. I look to the floor, thinking that it must have one of those floor flush things that you step on. Nope. Cautiously, I approach the toilet, wondering what I need to do. I peer in. I am…shocked. The reason there is no flush handle is that there is no need to flush. The toilet seat is essentially a large hole atop an excrement tank. There, about three feet below me, swirls gallons and gallons of human waste. Anything that I…produce will simply fall below and take its place in this American melting pot of sorts.

I now face a dilemma. I weigh my options and the possible outcomes. I could stand there and pee – but should the bus crash and overturn I would be in a sorry state. I could sit there and wait for that guy I am supposed to see about a horse – but then all it would take would be for the vehicle to go over a large bump or through a big pothole to cause an uprising below, for the substance below to wave up and lick my cheeks. I am against this possibility. I've always felt as a general rule that excrement should only need to be wiped off once – and then only from and by the producer. I can't go against my principles.

I decide on a third option. I stand as far back from the 'bowl' as possible – close to the door – and aim a long, direct stream. This will allow me a quick escape in the event that I hear the driver scream, or anything. It is not without its risks, though. Aiming straight, as 3 billion understand and another 3 billion refuse to believe, is notoriously difficult.

It's one thing to point a hose and fire. It's another to wrap the hose in a couple of centimetres of slippery, loose flesh and then try to aim. But the way I see it, I have no choice.

My journal entry from that day is quite interesting. It details an eight-step plan for using the bathroom on a Greyhound:

Methodology:
1) Stay as far away from toilet seat as possible.
2) Empty oneself into pit, having already stared down it in wonder.
3) Search for the flush handle.
4) Realise that there is none, as your waste has simply fallen into a pit.
5) Contemplate this.
6) Think of the 'flap' system on Irish trains, whereby the 'flush' handle is a mechanism that opens a 'flap' at the bottom of the toilet bowl and dumps the contents onto the tracks.
7) Write to various transport authorities.
8) Stare once more down pit.

I exit the bathroom, and return to my seat. Marie asks me if anything is wrong. I put on a brave face, and smile. What she will never know is that I am crying inside – I lost a little piece of myself forever into that dark and gurgling faeces pit – something I can never recover.

About an hour later, the bus comes over a hill in the Iron Range, and there, materialising before us, is Duluth, and Lake Superior. Duluth is built at the western end of Lake Superior – the largest freshwater lake in the world. It lies at a corner of the lake, where the southern shore abruptly ends, and the shoreline suddenly swings northeast. It is a thin city, grasping onto the lake's coastline for about twenty miles or so. It's a combination of rural, urban, industrial, seafaring and land-lubbin'. It is surrounded by hills to the South and by the lake to the northeast. It is a very pretty town, in a Mid-West kinda way. It is, to phrase it awkwardly, the Mid-West's 'East Coast USA'.

Soon, we arrive at the Greyhound station. It looks (and works) just like a gas station without the gas pumps. Marie's mom is there to greet us. I have finally made it to the centre of Marie's world.

***

The hills that overlook Duluth alternate between those that are bleak and red and those that are dressed in autumn colours. This creates an oddity in that the hills both complement and loom over the city at the same time. Atop one of these, overlooking the city, is Enger tower. It sits in a pretty, well kept park that offers spectacular views of the city and lake below. The tower is basically a viewing post – a few hundred steps bring you to the top from where one gets a 360° panorama.

It is the story behind the tower, however, that I find most interesting. Basically, when you cut to the heart of the story put out by the local tourist board, the tower was built around 1900 by a guy who wanted to build something to commemorate himself. Bert Enger's story is basically one of poor immigrant turned wealthy local man. Thus, here I have found a monument to the very promise of America itself. I ask some of the locals about Bert Enger and his story. They all say the same thing. 'Oh – he's the guy they named the tower after.' From the promise of America, we find the reality - it's no longer the case that the tower commemorates the great deeds of his life – it's that the commemoration becomes the only thing he is remembered for.

Which brings us to an interesting American cultural phenomenon – something that I find particularly endearing and likable about the country – an…eccentricity that is uniquely American. Many Americans feel that the world revolves around them – and I don't mean that in a derogatory way. What it does mean, however, is that far from being one nation of 300 million souls with one great national culture – or one national dream, at any rate – America is actually 300 million individual nations – each with its own cultures, ideologies and history. Every culture and society has its heroes and legends. These America idiocultures are no different. The guy who built Enger tower is a classic example of this mindset. A great man or woman need only be great in his or her own eyes to warrant cultural hero status. Thus, it is seen as perfectly legitimate that Bert Enger – no matter what his life story – might simply have built a tower to commemorate himself.

America is filled with hundreds of thousands of tiny, irreverent museums, statues and memorials. American culture, if it does exist, is made up of the symbols of thousands of idiocultures. Darwin, Minnesota is home to the world's largest ball of twine wound by a single person. Francis A. Johnson wound the twine for forty years as a memorial to himself, so that he could say 'Here's what I did with my life'.

Another classic example of the 'eccentric' crusading quality that is unique to America is the 'Museum of Questionable Medical Devices' in the Twin Cities, which we have the pleasure of visiting during my first month. It is a great collection of quack medical ideas collected obsessively by one man over the course of his lifetime. Europe, and Ireland, is lacking in such places – we dare to question the point and purpose of such displays. But to do so is to miss the point. Rather than try to figure out a purpose for everything and to see what we can learn, should we follow the American lead? These places are supported and treasured because they show us, simply, that everyone can have a cause of their own. No cause is better or worse than any other – be it the guy in New Jersey who spent his life carving a miniature New York City, the giant statue of a Troll eating a car under a bridge in Seattle, the Mustard museum in Wisconsin, or the insanity of Las Vegas. American culture is a passively grown, organic entity, to which everyone is invited to contribute, no matter how odd or outlandish their individual contribution is deemed to be. It is something that we have to an extent forgotten in Europe. Here, many of our cultural outlets – museums etc. are state sponsored, and tell an 'Official' story. We have become net consumers of culture – a far cry from the net producers of America.

The Museum of Questionable Medical Devices, for me, crystallises this trait. It is, essentially, a monument to this individualism, filled with the zany, but at one time accepted, ideas of delightful madmen. It is filled with an unusual number of sex devices used in the 19th century to quieten women, in asylums in particular. It also has bizarre diagnostic machines that needed no more than mailed handwriting samples to give an attempted diagnosis of syphilis, polio and smallpox.

My own personal favourite is an original, turn-of-the-century phrenology machine – a machine that tells you about yourself by reading the bumps on your skull and judging intelligence based on head size. I find, to my delight, that it still works. To my further delight, they offer to do a reading on me! I sit in the chair, and the large electronic helmet device is lowered onto my head. The machine is switched on. At the end, I receive a printout, detailing my personality traits, and a guide that I can use to divine my ideal job from the reading.

I hope that my ideal job might be something like 'writer', or 'journalist'. I am not averse to discovering that perhaps a political job lies in the bumps and nuances of my skull – I've always had a lot to say, and being paid for it might not be a bad thing. What would my ideal job be? I can hardly wait. I begin to read the printout. It is not quite what I expect. Would I be a great writer? Nope. Would I be a journalist? Nope. Would I be a politician? Nope. I am destined to be…a Zeppelin Attendant. Bet you don't see that one coming.

I am actually glad that it said 'Zeppelin Attendant'. It makes for a great pub story. I also find it ironic – I majored in Anthropology, which is about as useful on the jobs market as being a Zeppelin Attendant. That evening, I search several jobs databases, ready to wow potential Zeppelin Attendant employers with my phrenological readings. I even spent part of the previous summer in Friedrichshafen on Lake Constance in Germany, where the Zeppelin was first tested. I figure that I will let the rival employers vie with each other for my services – each offering more and more money for the right to employ me – the industry-relevant child of destiny. Alas, it is not to be. I am unable to find any Zeppelin-related job categories or sub-categories on any of the websites. I am destined to roam the world as a fraud – taking any job I can get to keep myself alive, unable to use my great gift – my curse, being born about seventy years too late.

What I get from this is my first whiff of what it must be to be an American. I am a potential Zeppelin Attendant. That is just eccentric and unique enough to be American. For the first time since I arrive, I feel that perhaps someday, I will merit a museum of my own.

***

I have not had the chance to do much shopping as yet in the USA – aside, that is, from daily trips to our local corner shop, the 8th Street Market. I have noticed that the Twin Cities have very little 'city shopping' – the kind that grows up organically in each city centre. Instead, all shopping is done at purpose-built, soulless malls.

My first real experience of such malls is in Duluth, the shopping capital of the area, attracting shoppers from all over the northern half of the State and adjoining areas in Canada. Miller Hill Mall is the place to be. So we go.

There is a big difference between mall shopping and city shopping – something more impersonal about it. Cities are full of narrow streets and alleyways that attract an eclectic mix of small, independent shops and restaurants. Half the joy of city shopping, for me at any rate, is simply being able to wander the streets and take it all in. This is something I find lacking in malls. First of all, without a car, the malls are not accessible – the bus system will get you close, but there are few sidewalks. Thus, strolling casually along the streets is relegated to simply hurrying through the car park, feeling low for not being able to afford a car.

Second of all, malls are planned – usually as enclosed streets. Thus, they lack the side streets. Generally, they lack independent shops – many of them being purpose-built by large multinationals who retain control over who the other residents of the mall will be. Lastly, they usually contain the same few predictable multinationals. Usually the only product individual to each mall is the price.

I find Miller Hill to be nothing out of the ordinary. It is large. It is predictable. I do my fair share of shopping, however – particularly at Barnes and Noble, my first experience with this particular chain. I enjoy it, but don't find anything that I can't find at any other mall west of the Atlantic.

I have, by now, begun to hear rumours: shopping rumours. The reason that the Twin Cities lacks a shopping soul is because of the Mall of America – a mall so large that it forced the commercial dereliction of the city centres. I do not believe them. No mall – no matter how large – could force the closure of two entire city centres, forcing them to re-invent themselves as locations for corporate headquarters.

Asked about my Miller Hill experience, I respond that I think it to be unnecessarily big. I am informed that I haven't seen the Mall of America yet.

"Is it much bigger?" I ask, naively.

Marie and I decide to take a day and go to the Mall. By now, I am intrigued – just how big could it be? On the internet, I find out that it gets more visitors each year than the Grand Canyon, Empire State Building and Statue of Liberty combined. Hmm…Sounds pretty big!

We decide to go in the week following our Duluth trip. The point of the Duluth trip is to attend what turned out to be a very successful Thanksgiving. There's no point delving into the details, save to say that family seems to be the same the world over. Every now and again, we get together, and remember both the reasons we get together so infrequently and why it is we wish we could get together more often.

Thanksgiving marks the official beginning of the Christmas season. This fact in itself I find to be refreshing. In Ireland, I had seen a couple of Christmas ads before I left – and I left in September! Now that Thanksgiving is behind us, we can go to the Mall and see the capitalist feeding frenzy that attacks for but one season each year.

Back in Minneapolis, we catch the No. 3 bus, and are on our way.

Public transport in America is…odd. I find the service to be both infrequent and expensive. The bus company doesn't have the capacity to expand for rush hour, so they actually put the price up by 50 per cent during these times, to dissuade people from using it!

We are on our way to the Minneapolis suburb of Bloomington – now itself almost as large as either of the Twin Cities, due in no small part to the presence of a certain monster shopping mall. The bus drives out past the Airport, and up Snelling Avenue. We are close.

"There it is," says Marie, as she points out the window.

'Hmm,' I think. 'Doesn't seem so big. In fact, I think I've seen bigger.'

Turns out though that I hadn't. The structure that I see is merely the parking lot.

We alight from the bus deep inside the bowels of the Mall – at a purpose built transit centre. We find an elevator, and began our ascent. Suddenly, we are in the Mall. There are flashing lights. There are neon signs. There are brand symbols. There are price tags. There is food. It is…is…overwhelming. I honestly do not know what to do. Everywhere I look, a hundred brands and prices compete with each other for my attention. I do not know which one to concentrate on. It is too much to take in.

We take a map from an information booth. The Mall, it seems, has three levels. The top level even has a cinema and nightclub complex. Each floor has a massive food court, where it is possible eat as many brands as one could handle – although, strangely, no McDonalds. Most amazing of all – in the centre of the square mall stands…Camp Snoopy, a full-scale theme park named after Minnesota's most famous fictional dog. This is matched in scale only by the full-scale aquarium in the basement – complete with Great White sharks and all! This really is more monster than mall. It's no exaggeration to think that if the Mall doesn't have it, it doesn't exist outside of your mind.

We walk around. It is colossal. Here, however, I find what has been lacking in other malls. There are small, independent shops next door to multinational conglomerates. It is possible to ramble: there is probably more street space here than in all of Dublin city centre! There are people walking – not driving – from store to store. And the selection is both eclectic and unpredictable. Just the way I like it.

However, I don't like all of it. Never an easy man to please, I find fault even here. The problem is the fact that it is still a mall. It is designed specifically as a mall. It is designed to sell. Thus it is a marketer's paradise. Every square inch has been pondered and considered according to profit. There are too many competing messages. There are too many stimuli. In a city, there is not that pre-planned, clinical feel. Shops and businesses occupy buildings rather than cold, warehouse-type open spaces. A building without a shop is still a building. It can be pretty to look at – or not. It is in itself an integral part of the cityscape. A shop lot in a mall without a shop is just an open space. If it is not being filled with the activities of profit, it is cold and lonely. It does not exist in its own right. It is this more than anything that makes me prefer city shopping to mall shopping. It is also the one element that I feel architects and designers have struggled even to recognise to date. It is also one of the main reasons that I feel isolated in soulless American downtowns. Efficient, purpose-built units have a soul different to the type I recognise.

I'm going to put my neck out here and prove that I am at best a poet and at worst a whacko. Shopping is, in Europe, an art form. In America, however, it is more a necessity. True art needs to be displayed in the correct frame and in the correct space to allow full and proper appreciation. Galleries are usually imposing places – where the art on display is treated with reverence. So too with European shopping. The shop is as important as the product. Thus, more thought has been traditionally expended on setting – even though this seems to be changing for efficiency. In America, shops are functional, because shopping is not an art form. Thus, the Mall of America – a shrine to shopping – is in itself designed to be more like a functional warehouse than a city centre – even though that's essentially what it's supposed to be. There is nothing more to it.

***

We Irish, like the British and many of our other European neighbours, love to talk about the weather. We complain about it constantly. One day of rain in a month of sunshine is usually an ideal catalyst. It is true, however, that a month of sunshine is something that I don't think Ireland has ever experienced in its two billion or so years of geographic existence.

Usually, it rains. In summer, the beautiful, beating sunshine and searing heat are blocked by active rain clouds. Heavy winter snowfall – the type that beautifies much of the European continent at Christmas – is non-existent in Ireland. It's not that the snow doesn't fall – the snow that falls just hasn't frozen yet. In the springtime newborn lambs and calves have a constant wet pelt and muddy feet due to the abundant precipitation – April showers and all that. Autumn is, but for the incessant rainfall, as dry as the other seasons. In fact, the only sure-fire way to check the season is to look at a calendar.

It was a rainy day when I left Ireland for America in mid-September. It was a hot, dusty day when I stepped off the plane and into Minneapolis-St Paul airport on the same day. There is not much talk of weather in America – not that I find, at any rate. There is no need for it. In Ireland, the temperature can hover around the zero mark in winter. We complain about it to each other. In Minnesota, the weather gets much, much colder. It does all of the talking, leaving no need to point it out.

Example one. In early December, I tell Marie that I will meet her after work. We plan to go to Annie's in Dinkytown for a burger and a malt. She works about twenty-five minutes away by foot.

"I'll walk down to meet you after work," I say.

"Walk? Are you crazy? Do you know how cold it is out there?"

Do I take her advice? Nope. I have a beard. My brother has taken to introducing me to people as Maximus, Commander of the Armies of the North – you get the idea of the type of beard it is. I leave the building and begin to walk. Within five minutes, the cold is stabbing my exposed skin. I become a little panicky now, worrying that it might be colder than I can handle. Then I remember the day that I was delayed for two hours in a train station in Sigmaringen in Southern Germany in temperatures of -11°C. It surely can't be as cold as that – and I came through that fine. So on I trudge. Five minutes later, I notice something – but do not fully realise what it is for a few minutes more. When I open my mouth, the skin on my face is sore – as if being pinched. The reason? Little *icicles* have formed in my beard. When I open my mouth, the beard bristles pull. 'Now is a good time to panic,' I think.

I place a gloved hand over my beard in a vain attempt to defrost it and to keep it so until I make it to the restaurant. When I arrive, I go straight into the bathroom and splash warm water over my beard, thus completing the defrostation – a word that is, oddly enough, the correct word to use to describe the destruction of trees through use of low temperatures. Poor joke, I know. That night, I look at the weather forecast. The temperature that day was -25°C.

Example two. I arrange to meet a friend at the No. 3 bus stop – about a five- or six-minute walk from the house – and go to the Mall of America. I bid Marie farewell, and headed to the door.

"Where do you think you're going without a hat?"

I have long resisted wearing hats. It is not something I do at home and, therefore, however irrational it may seem, do not want to do it there. I tell Marie that I'll be fine – that I'll have only to brave the cold for five or six minutes before I get on the bus and then on to a nice warm mall. She protests. I do not listen.

In all of my life, I have never felt cold like this. Within two minutes I am in full panic mode. My beard has quickly frozen over. My ears go so numb that I am seriously worried about losing them. The feeling in my ears does not totally come back until later that night, *after* I arrive home. My hair freezes into hair-cicles. Weirdest and most worrisome of all, my jeans began to freeze, and burn my legs when they touch the material. Ever since this day, I wear whatever the locals recommend. Oh – and the temperature that day? It's -40° – where Celsius and Fahrenheit meet!!

Incidentally, I've heard that Kofi Annan has a similar story about refusing to wear a hat when he was a student in Minneapolis. He apparently quickly learned, as I did, that the locals are usually right about these things.

It is so cold here in winter that the streets literally become deserted. There are five miles of tunnels connecting the downtown buildings together so that people don't have to brave the cold. I've said that people don't complain about the cold – and this is true. It is just so cold that it wouldn't do any good. But what they do in place of complaining is to collect weather anecdotes. And they are great. Apparently, November/December is not even the coldest part of winter – that isn't until February. The girl that I am going to the Mall of America to meet tells me of a February a few years back when a flight she was on couldn't take off because the antifreeze had frozen.

The weather, however, helps me to understand something about the fashion sense in Minnesota. I had considered the fashions here to be a little…off. Things don't really match. Coats are large, and ugly. I now begin to realise the rules. First of all, wear everything you have during winter. Secondly, buy the biggest coat you can damn well afford – the type that's just too big to ever look good, no matter who the designer is. Minnesota in winter is full of walking clothes piles. Only tiny, tiny eye-slits in the facial area give away the fact that the clothes do not have their own life force – but actually contain human beings.

For me, the amazing thing is the fact that these cities are just over a century old. Someone actually went there, experienced the six (yes, six) months of winter, and thought 'Gee – what a great place to found a city!'

And it's not just the cold – it's also the snow. Now, I know that it probably seems a bit obvious – cold and snow go together. But it is the type of snow that is astounding. Before my American sojourn, Marie and I were watching an episode of David Attenborough's *Life in the Freezer* series. The particular episode dealt with the penguin mating cycle. We watched the screen as thousands upon thousands of penguins huddle together – standing in a group for months, bracing the sharp, biting Antarctic gales. You know the scene: wind sweeping across the snowfields – a classic Antarctic vista.

"Hey – that's like January in Minnesota," says Marie. She is not kidding.

The summers are the complete opposite. It is not unknown for the temperatures to reach 40°C – the type of weather where all that's possible to do is to put your kids into the refrigerator and freeze your underwear.

It's not just temperature that's 'big'. Other weather is equally huge and impressive. Take storms, for example. I thought that I had experienced true 'storms' back in Ireland. I had, after all, lived through the great Dublin electrical storm of 1984. I had experienced Hurricane Charlie in 1987. I had even been stuck in a car with my screaming grandmother during a huge electrical storm in Wexford in 1991. I know what big weather is. Or, at least, I think I do. Before I went to America, Marie told me that I had not experienced a true storm. I protested vehemently. Since returning, I have remained quiet on the subject. The great Dublin electrical storm was not so great, it turns out. Hurricane Charlie was little more than a piddle fest. The Wexford storm is the kind of thing that I'm sure that parents in America rent out to entertain the kids at birthday parties.

The scene: there are five of us in the car, driving back from visiting friends in Rochester, Minnesota (home of the famous Mayo clinic). The toothless radio lounges on an old rocking chair on the back porch. 'Storm's a comin',' it says.

We decide to leave early – just in case. Or, at least, everyone else has decided. I can't understand what the big deal is. I have seen storms. In fact, a car is one of the safest places to be – the rubber tyres mean that there's less chance of injury should the car be struck by lightning. I share my thoughts.

There is no comment.

I now know that everyone was thinking:

'Fat lot of good your tyres will do you when the car is picked up by a tornado, or swept away in a flood.'

I should point out at this stage that although we do encounter the storm, it was, for us, incident free. It was also, however, one of the most awesome sights that I have ever encountered.

The storm is always close – but never hits us. It seems to be about ten miles away to our right for the entire duration of our journey home. This is in itself an amazing sight. Picture a plain before a mountain range – a site where flat land suddenly gives birth to raised leviathans. This is how the storm looks. To our right, it begins abruptly. It has definable borders. It is monstrous. Although it is night, we can see it perfectly. There is an almost constant stream of lightning – but the kind that looks more like fire than electricity. I am awestruck.

I would have other experiences with equally fearsome weather. On one occasion Marie, her sister and I are about to return to where we are staying after a day in Miller Hill Mall, where I am spending not cash, but hypocrisy with gay abandon. We enter the parking lot. It is dark – about four or so hours before the sun is due to set. What is weirder still is the smell in the air – a smell of 'darkness' that I have never before encountered. There is an eerie chill in the warm air. 'Must be a rainstorm coming to clear the summer air,' I think.

I jump into the back seat, and the girls into the front. We are off. I look out of the window to see if the rain is coming. I look all around, but cannot discern which clouds will be the ones to break. Then, strange things begin to happen. The wind begins to blow the clouds. Nothing strange there – except for the fact that the wind is blowing the clouds *apart*. The clouds are being pulled asunder like cotton candy at a carnival – each piece is blowing away in a different direction! I have never seen anything like this!

Gertie and Marie are equally intrigued as to what is going on. Suddenly, it clicks. The girls look at each other and say, at the same time, 'Tornado'. They smile, happy that they have at last solved the mystery.

Tornado? The words bring an extra wind – this time from my trousers, as I begin the process of shitting myself. Being Irish, I have but limited experience of tornadoes. In fact, I have no experience outside of the famous few deemed handsome enough to be able to land parts in major pictures, such as the looker in *Twister*, or *The Wizard of Oz* pin-up. It had not escaped my attention either that these tornadoes usually played quite destructive roles in the movies. They never land roles in romantic comedies or Hugh Grant movies. Thus, when I hear that a tornado is coming, I tend to run away, rather than hang around to see if I can get an autograph.

Being an unashamed coward, I begin to panic. And then, just to pour salt into the wounds, it begins to rain so hard that the car windscreen quickly turns from transparent, through translucent, to opaque. We have to pull over. As far as I can tell, we are tornado fodder.

The girls try to calm me, saying that a tornado cone had not fully touched down in Duluth for forty years. It turns out that they are right. No tornado would touch down in Duluth that day. However – one would touch down in Superior, Wisconsin, about ten miles away across the State Line. The tornadoes are here – and they'd be staying to play a full season.

In the Twin Cities, tornado warnings take the form of alarms – similar to the air-raid sirens used to clear city streets during World War II. When I first heard it, I was in a car stuck in a traffic jam. The woman in the car behind gets such a fright that she rear-ends us. I am worried. There are five of us in the car. We have all just spent the day at Valley Fair amusement park having a great time.

I have seen the movies. It is either the happy, unsuspecting people who are enjoying life too much or the oul' bastard that no one likes that end up being taken by the tornado. I am not yet an oul' bastard. But I have spent the day enjoying life to the full – something I had not been doing when the threat of a tornado struck Duluth. I am suddenly a prime candidate for tornado rage!

Sure enough, no fewer than *four* tornadoes touched down that day.

We tune into the local news to get updates. There is one heading right for us. We are sitting ducks. It is tense – especially with the sirens going off. And to make it worse – when we open the car door to inspect the damage from the minor traffic accident we are involved in, the smell of darkness wafts through my nostrils for only the second time in my life.

Luckily, however, the tornado peters out before it comes any closer to us. The other three tornadoes take off in different directions. They end up hitting rural areas – farms and the like. Sounds to me like they are only teenage tornadoes – probably all boozed up and looking to cause a little mischief – nothing more. The only twister that I would experience that day would be in my underpants, which have twisted into a ropey knot due to my heightened state of anxiety.

CHAPTER THREE

Seattle

A friend of ours, studying dance in Cornish – a school in Seattle, Washington – has invited me out to stay with her for a few days. Sounds like a good idea – a chance to see more of this vast land. Marie, who is in the middle of writing her final thesis, decides against making the trip.

I log on to the internet to search for flights. I am looking for the American equivalent of Ryanair, hoping that I can get to Seattle for less than the price of a dollar – which, incidentally, is somewhere around the dollar mark. I stumble across the website for Frontier Airlines – practically the only airline offering budget airfares from Minnesota. What, then, will American budget airfare cost? America likes to do everything big, so I am expecting a situation whereby the airlines might *pay* me for my custom. It turns out that I am right about America doing everything big. The cheapest I can get for a return flight to Seattle is $300. I check some of the bigger airlines – turns out that Frontier is the cheapest by a long shot. One company even quotes me $1500. To put this into perspective – the return trans-Atlantic flights that brought me to Minnesota in the first place had cost less than $400.

So, in early November, we brave the snow and ice – wearing a hat, of course. Marie drops me off at the airport. Well, actually, Marie drops me off at my gate – it was still practically possible for non-passengers to walk you to your seat in those days. Soon, we are airborne. It will not be a direct flight – the best I could manage is to book Seattle via Denver.

I have a window seat – I usually do. The views fascinate me. It also intrigues me to be able to see the tops of the clouds rather than just merely their underbellies. Being from Ireland, I've spent many damp hours walking around inside street-level clouds. The airplane view simply completes the picture.

The Minneapolis to Denver leg of the journey is virtually cloud-free, however, and I get to see a good bit of the landscape. I can see fields soon after take-off – big fields – bigger than anything back home. They are all square fields – perfect squares, with massive circles cut into them – as if the farmers of the Mid-West are all involved in a celebration of Da Vinci and have only to fit a proportionate man into the geometric shapes (Vitruvian Man). I never do find out what type of farming or crop requires this circular…attention. Nor do I want to know, as it's probably something quite banal. The landscape does not break during the entire flight.

Earlier, I talked about seeing a great storm – about seeing how it rose into the sky like a great mountain range. Now, looking out of the plane window, I see an actual mountain range – the Rockies – that great mountainous spine stretching from Alaska to Tierra del Fuego, before re-emerging to form the Antarctic Peninsula. And it is spectacular. It quite literally rises to majestic proportions out of nothing. All the way from Minnesota, the ground below could have been used by spirit-level manufacturers to test their wares. Suddenly, the ground is suitable for testing only by insane spirit-level manufacturers. The plane now swoops down into Denver airport.

Now, I spend a total of about ten minutes actually *in* Denver airport – and that includes the return journey. The plane arrives late, causing the connecting flight to be delayed. Thus, we are hurried – actually running – through the building. This aside, I have to say that I like Denver airport. It is one of the few American airports that I've been in that does not follow the usual plan. From the outside, it looks like a giant tent. The roof itself has as many peaks as the nearby Rockies. Its slight eccentricity gives it an appealing allure.

Despite having to rush from plane to plane, I do find time – nay, make time – to use the bathroom. I look for the picture of the little black urine guy whose image graces more doors than any other.

(By the way – ever noticed that the three bathroom symbols are 'man', 'woman' and 'wheelchair'? Apparently being disabled is a gender all by itself – which is an interesting social comment.)

I follow the signs, and find the bathroom. But the little man is not alone. He is joined in his symbolism by…a little tornado! Instantly, I understand. Tornadoes are notorious for swallowing things up. This is obviously where they come to…get rid of the excess. As I reach for the door, I fully expect to see a tornado swirling about in a urinal and another trying to plug his electric razor into a socket at the wash hand basin. I open the door. No tornadoes. There is, however, a yellow sign, indicating that this bathroom doubles as a tornado shelter. I am about as far from home culturally as I am geographically.

Soon, we are on our way again. I am looking forward to seeing more of the Rockies from the air. But, alas, it is not to be. The second leg of the journey has anything but clear skies. Two and a half grey hours later, the plane lands in Seattle-Tacoma airport. I have made it. The first Carabini to the Pacific.

'My parents will be so proud,' I think.

Turns out they are more indifferent than proud when I call them with the news.

A very odd thing happened on another airline flying to Seattle around the time of my journey. This is a true story – feel free to look it up in news reports from October 2000. I'll recount it as best I can without embellishing it. It seems that a woman needed to fly to Seattle, but suffered a heart condition that could deteriorate if she was exposed to stress. The solution? Why, a 300 lb stress-reducing pig, of course! The pig was even allowed to fly – for free – in First Class! The pig apparently caused a little bit of bother on the flight, when it tried to get into the cockpit and then went to the galley, refusing to leave until fed. Doesn't seem like an anti-stress variety of pig to me. Still, though – no heart attack – so the pig must have done its job. Nobody likes stress, but then, we can't all afford to keep a 300 lb pig around either. I myself try to find a compromise, and briefly consider carrying a packet of sausages and a side of bacon with me.

***

For the first time during my stay, I am a proper tourist. Thus, I do not have to make as big an effort: there is a difference in approach between living with a people and visiting a people. I arrive on the Friday night. The Saturday will be Seán's big day out in Seattle.

I wake at 8.30 a.m. My host, and her roommate, are both up and both cooking their breakfasts. It is a pleasant apartment – very modern, very clean. But it is also very small. Thus, as I am sleeping in the living area, they are essentially cooking around me. A stranger would think that they are preparing me to be cooked – and perhaps they were, until I awoke, forcing them to change tack.

"Do you want breakfast, Seán?"

I do – but don't want to tell them. The reason? That damn smiling black woman on the pancake mix box is back – I have tasted her culinary quackery before.

It turns out that the girls need not have asked me whether or not I wanted breakfast. They make it for me anyway. But they have been creative. Into the wet pancake batter they mix a bag of chocolate chips. And they taste good.

Our first stop of the day is to visit the Space Needle – Seattle's most widely known icon, a remnant of the 1962 World's Fair exhibition. I want to walk – looks close enough from where we are – and besides – I'll get to see more of the city. Off we set on a grey, overcast morning.

Turns out the Space Needle is indeed close – but only in the grand scheme of things. An hour after setting out, having walked down the straightest, longest avenue that side of the Mississippi, we arrive at the Needle. Better be worth it.

And it is. It looks exactly like it does on TV – like it belongs in an episode of *The Jetsons*. I like it. We take the elevator to the top – bypassing the revolving restaurant, of course. I've never understood the appeal. Dublin has the right idea when it comes to revolving restaurants. It has none, but each eatery is filled with drunken clientele whose inebriated state gives them the impression that the restaurant is revolving.

Soon, we are at the top, looking out over Seattle and Puget Sound. It all looks really beautiful. I don't know what it is about viewpoints that makes them so popular. They seem to satisfy a deep, unknown need within us. My brother once told me that he reckoned he could cash in on the Irish tourism boom by constructing a massive elevator shaft from which Dublin city could be viewed. It wouldn't even have to look nice, or have a nice name to make money. He even suggested that it could be made from asbestos and nobody would care. I think he has a good idea there.

This is my first time at an American viewing tower. It is different to what I am used to. The main reason for this is the street grid system – all parallel, all in blocks. It gives it a slightly unappealing aspect – makes the whole thing seem a little too manmade and over planned. There is a tour guide on hand to explain the view to us. She starts out by telling us that the view from the title character's apartment in *Frasier* could only exist if he lived in a TV transmitter tower that overlooks the city. The Space Needle is not downtown – it is quite separate from the other high-rise buildings in Seattle.

Afterwards, we take the Seattle Monorail from the Needle to downtown. We make our way to the historic district around Pioneer Square. It is a nice area to ramble around, so we ramble. We stumble upon a museum near Occidental Park, dedicated to the Klondike Gold Rush. It is a fascinating little place, filled with the stories and artefacts of the tens of thousands of gold prospectors who came through Seattle in the 19th century on their way to the Klondike to find their fortune. It is a sad place. Steely, broken eyes look out from every black and white photo. They seem to look at only me. Although I don't know what it is they are trying to tell me, I understand on a level deeper than my own consciousness. They are in pursuit of something. That is enough.

Our next stop is the massively enjoyable Seattle Underground. Seattle was originally built at too low a level for flush toilets to work. To counter this, the city authorities in the late-19th century actually raised the street levels. This meant that what was the ground floor is now the basement, and what was once the first floor is now the ground floor. Entire streets became preserved in this way. They are now collectively known as the Underground. The Underground unfolds the story of Seattle in a very entertaining, human way, essentially putting the economic development of the city down to prostitution. I'm sure that most cities have a similar story to tell, and would but for the politically correct language of officialdom, where history for some reason has to be clean and uninteresting before it can be publicised.

That afternoon, I take a guided boat tour of the harbour. My friend has to go rehearse for an upcoming show, so I go alone. The guide on the tour is…great – although I suspect that neither he nor anyone else on board knows it. He is in his late thirties, desperately boring and overweight. I suspect that the only woman in his life might be a certain black woman with a permanent smile – and they'd been seeing far too much of each other. He is a nerd. He obviously takes an unhealthy interest in the activities of the harbour. He is dressed in a navy sweater – 'navy' both in colour and style! He begins the tour by telling us the statistics of the mighty vessel upon which we will be sojourning. He knows the name of every vessel in port – and in Seattle, that's no mean feat. Not only that – he knows what cargo most of the ships are carrying and the timetable they keep! Within five minutes, the rest of the passengers are either soundly asleep or contemplating suicide. I am the exception – I am lapping it up. About half way through the tour, he suddenly becomes animated.

"Oh – oh – look! Look!" he shouts excitedly, flailing his arms in a particular direction. "Here's a treat for us – something we haven't been expecting!"

Apparently, the ship carrying a cargo of Toyota cars from Japan has arrived a day ahead of schedule. That is the big deal. All around me, people who have briefly roused from their slumber to cock an eye to see what he is talking about fall back to asleep, disgruntled at the fact that he has dared to show some enthusiasm.

After an hour, we arrive back at the pier. I buy fish and chips and share them with a seagull – the biggest seagull I have ever seen. We sit together, watching the world and the day go by. I take his picture. Every now and again, I take it out to look at it. And every time I do, I'm reminded of something very poignant: some seagulls really are huge.

That night I go to see some contemporary dance at a local theatre. It is absolutely fascinating and beautiful to watch, but I must admit that I have not a clue as to what the hell they are trying to communicate. As far as I can tell, the dancers have worms, and are trying to get rid of them through yoga. Not much of a storyline, I know – but they manage to get two hours out of it.

***

Seattle has one of the prettiest settings of any town I have encountered – be it in America or elsewhere. It sits on a peninsula jutting into Puget Sound, which looks to be a bay under construction. On one side, the Pacific. On the other, Mount Rainier – a close neighbour of Mount St Helens, both peaks snow-capped and beautiful. Seattle is a large enough city – about a million or so live in the metro area, making it comparable in size to Dublin. It makes its money from Microsoft and Boeing.

Now, I liked Seattle. I regard it as one of my favourite places, despite having been there only once. The reason for this is that I feel more at home here than in the Mid-West. Much of it feels familiar to me. For example, chips – not fries – are bought from small stands around the harbour. Sweets are sold instead of candy in many places. And, most importantly of all, it still retains a functioning downtown.

Seattle is a bit of a paradoxical place, but in a way that highlights the paradoxes that exist in America in general. Although a wealthy city due to the presence of the two local corporate powerhouses, it does not draw its dynamism and spirit from them. Instead, its spirit can be found at Pike Place, the famous fish market, or in its thriving downtown full of independent shops, such as Ye Old Curiosity Shop – which displays, among other things, the dried-out body of an 1850s cowboy who was found in the desert.

I am staying in an apartment on Capitol Hill – a likable city district that is home to every section of society – the homeless, the eccentric, the student, the collared (blue, white and none). I hang out with my host's dance student friends, and have a really good time. I get to see a rehearsal of an upcoming show. To my surprise and delight, there are two reporters from local newspapers there covering the piece.

I like a town that likes art – no matter how 'good' or 'bad' it is. And when it comes to public art, Seattle is a Mecca. The Fremont district in particular is of note. There are unusual public sculptures all over. A gigantic troll sits under a freeway bridge, eating a Volkswagen Beetle. Lenin stands on a street corner, eternally pondering his next words. Downtown, a huge three-storey Hammering Man acts as town blacksmith, raising and lowering his right hand all day with the eagerness of a male adolescent. A bus stop shelter is filled with eternally waiting statues.

The soul of Seattle is very much alive and independent, which is why it seems a very unlikely place to hold a G8 meeting, as happened in 1999. I am in Seattle a year after the now famous Battle of Seattle, where the public got together and sent a message to the powerful. The message was simple, and not a new one in America. It is a message that Presidents past have built their legacies upon: 'A Square Deal for All'. What is so wrong with that? Walking around Seattle and talking to the Seattleites, it is obvious that the city is still hurting.

At the conference, the powerful essentially did not listen, and turned on the crowd. 'How dare you protest at all. Don't you realise how powerful we are?' This is the message that reached the public that day. Even more worrisome, another message is sent, one that has been sent at every such encounter since; that peaceful protests will be ignored. What exactly are the powerful trying to do by ignoring and refusing to engage with the peaceful?

A few assholes in the crowd started rioting – just a handful out of the tens of thousands there. The police over-reacted. My friend, who is a good half-hour's walk away from the protest on Capitol Hill tells me that the police even came up to the Hill and randomly threw tear gas down alleys and onto deserted residential streets.

One of the great pillars of American society is the right to peaceful protest. If you don't agree with something, you have the right to say why. If you don't agree with an action, you have the right to let 'them' know. Seems fair enough. But this is changing. Rapidly. People who protest are labelled as 'whackos'. The word 'liberal' is actually an insult in America. This really sad state of affairs reinforces the impression that America is changing beyond recognition, and has almost come full circle. After all – America was *founded* as a protest. It was founded by a group of New England Liberals, whose loyalty lay not with any nation, but with a new sense of true freedom, for which America was a symbol. The very existence of America is in itself a symptom of the desire for a Square Deal, as Teddy Roosevelt so aptly put it.

But things have changed at the top. America's ruling class now behave like any old European monarchy. In fact, in recent times, the Presidents have been related to European royalty – take the Bush family, for example, and their cousins (albeit somewhat distant) in Buckingham Palace. Wealth lies in the hands of few, and poverty is the lot of many. America, founded on the idea that every person should have a Square Deal has become an America where every person has the right to a square deal so long as they can afford it. This subtle change – one that is not yet actively noticed by the masses – defines a new America. The Battle of Seattle is not the violence-filled orgy that a sensationalist media sought to portray. It was the ghosts of Jefferson and Washington come back to question what has happened. And they are tear-gassed.

Seattle, for me, will always be a symbol of how America *can* work. The city is alive. The arts are alive. The people are alive. The business community is alive. And – whether they know it or not – they get on relatively well, although there are many who dispute this. America could do worse than use the Seattle blueprint as the urban aspiration for the rest of the country.

***

I left for Seattle on 8 November 2000 – the day after the Presidential election. America is hooked on politics, and there is a civil war is playing out in the media. George W. Bush is on TV calling for the counting of the votes to stop and for Al Gore to concede. Bush has boils on his face – some covered with bright blue band-aids, some not. Al Gore is not on TV as much as he should be; he hasn't prepared for this. He has been too busy over the past few months trying to convince America that they should vote for someone who bears a striking similarity to Seymour Skinner on *The Simpsons*. And he has convinced them. That still doesn't mean that he is going to win, though.

I've long been a political junkie. In fact, I come from a long line of political junkies. I've even been known to stay up late to watch the returns from the Welsh Assembly elections. For me, it's an addiction for which I brave the apathetic wilderness of society to locate my fix. The prospect of an American Presidential Election taking place while I am there is very appealing to me. The debates, the rallies, the votes, the counting: I can't wait. I know that it will play a big part in my stay. Little do I know *how* big.

First of all, let me try to explain a little about American politics. Broadly speaking, it is a two-party system, with the Republicans and the Democrats. Occasionally, a few others make it through, such as former pro-wrestler Jesse Ventura, an independent Governor of Minnesota. There are three branches of government – the Legislature (Congress), including the Senate and House of Representatives (two senators, and about one congressman per half a million people), the Executive (the President – more of this later) and the Judiciary (Supreme Court and other courts), who although technically separate from the Government are nominated by them. (It would be crass of me to simplify the American political divide as consisting of the Libertarians, whose followers vote Republican, and the Greens, whose followers vote Democrat – so I won't mention it!)

American elections are dirty. There is no moral high ground. In fact, taking the high ground usually just exposes you for all below to see. Advertisements are hilariously provocative. In 2000, there are many offices up for election – to every branch of officialdom one can imagine. The first ad that I see highlights the tactics. An incumbent Minnesotan congressman – Congressman Luther, I think, supports a limited prescription drug plan for seniors. Basically, if you're retired and need medicine, the plan would pay some of the costs. Seems fair enough, right? Wrong. The right to healthcare is not guaranteed in America. In fact there are some 40 million Americans without it. The reasons are manifold, including cost and the fact that many don't think that their taxes should pay for someone else's medical bills.

Now, agree with it or not, the financial argument can be made in a cogent manner. It can be quite a compelling argument if delivered correctly. But this is not the argument that Luther's political enemies choose to put forward. Instead, they argue that the plan will mean that the elderly would have no choice with the drugs they need because the government have control over the payments. Pure nonsense. But the slogan used on the ad is a classic. It doesn't say, 'We think that there's another way'. It doesn't say, 'We think that Congressman Luther is wrong'. It *does* say the following:

(in a sleazy voice) 'Tell Congressman Luther to stop scaring seniors.'

Don't you just love it? The idea that this guy wants to be elected purely so that he can indulge in his senior citizen scaring fetish is farcical. But that is what the main message used against him for the entire election turns out to be. He is elected in the end – but only by a very slim margin.

One day, sitting waiting for Marie at the University of Minnesota campus, I hear a ruckus outside the window. It is a small political protest. They are protesting the fact that Ralph Nader, the Green Party candidate for President, is not allowed join the televised debate between the two main candidates. Seemed like a fair gripe. The protest is less than dignified, however. First of all, they hold it in an obscure corner of the University – where no publicity can be garnered whatsoever! Second of all – the guy leading the protest – the 'Let Nader Debate' guy with the megaphone – is dressed as a giant yellow chicken. There is another guy dressed as Abraham Lincoln – an odd choice given that Abe is himself one of the founders of the two-party system.

An American student reading in the chair next to me leans over.

"Who's Nader?" she asks.

I explain.

"Gee – your accent! Where are you from?"

"Ireland."

"Wow – my family is Irish."

I instantly lose all respect for her, her American accent and her American parentage, and return to viewing the chicken protest. But she persists. I want to ask her how someone with *her* accent can consider themselves Irish, but she speaks first.

"You wanna go out some time?"

I decline. There will be no reuniting of the clans.

In the end, the heroic efforts of Abe and the Chicken would prove fruitless: Nader does not debate. Perhaps they should have tried something bigger than an obscure fancy dress protest.

I am looking forward to the debates. There will be three in total. I call everyone I know in America, and invite them over to watch the first on TV. Soon, the big day comes, and I am sitting on the sofa alone. 'No matter,' I think to myself, and go into the kitchen to make some microwave popcorn.

I set the timer for an hour to cook my five-minute popcorn. It doesn't really matter, because I usually stand around and wait until it stops popping. Around and around the popcorn bag goes – inflating with popped kernels and the smoky, broken dreams of germination. I stand in the kitchen door, face to the TV, back to the microwave.

On comes Bush. *Boo!* He gives a lame opening speech. On comes Gore. *Hooray!* He also gives a lame speech – mainly because the election is, by now, being fought around the same few apathetic issues. By now, both opening speeches have been made, and the questions begin.

Oh feck! My popcorn!

I run to the microwave, but it is too late. As I open the door, smoke billows forth, engulfing the kitchen and setting off the smoke alarm. As the initial billow clears, I can see something else – something that is neither smoke nor popcorn. It is fire. *Feck.* A thin blue flame haunts around the edges of the charred popcorn bag.

Thinking as fast as my popcorn-starved brain is capable, I grab the metal barbecue tongs hanging nearby. Using them, I pick up the burning bag, and run to the back door, where I fling it out onto the small landing of the fire escape. I throw snow on top of it.

I return to the kitchen to inspect the damage. Luckily, there is none. But there is a smell – a smell of burnt – no, charred – popcorn with a hint of the chemically treated paper bag. It is pretty nasty. I take a damp cloth and run it over the inside of the machine. It still stinks. I take some all-purpose cleaner, put it on the cloth, and scrub. Stink city. I take some bleach, and wipe it over the area. No effect whatsoever. I take a cup of water and lemon and put it into the microwave for two minutes, thinking that the steam might clean it. It doesn't. I do the only other thing I can. I leave the door open, and return to the debate. It is coming to a close. *Damn popcorn.*

Soon, I heard the back door open. Marie is home.

"Seán – why is there a bag of burnt popcorn at the back door? And why does the place stink?"

Three months later Marie's friend, who had been in Ecuador for the entire duration of my USA trip, would return to her apartment. She too would open the microwave oven and ask why it stank like burnt popcorn. The same question will be asked well into late summer.

What a great debate it has been! Much more exciting than anything back home. Altogether, a very memorable evening.

CHAPTER FOUR

Snows

It is snowing in Minnesota. The snows start on Hallowe'en, as Marie and I walk the Mississippi Mile. We watch as the city slowly begins to change colour. Leaves that have turned brown fall onto dull sidewalks. Snow will, in turn, fall upon the leaves. The streets fill with mulch. Over the coming weeks (to be more precise, over the coming days) the mulch will freeze. More snow will fall, creating a pristine blanket – but it will not remain pristine for long. The last few straggling leaves fall from the trees. Insects succumb to the falling temperature, their bodies landing upon the snow. Sludge from the road spatters onto it. And the squirrels bury the last of their food for the winter.

Apartments and houses close windows that have been open all summer long. They will remain closed until the thaw at the end of spring, opening only sporadically to air out the smell of an underwalked pet, or to tackle the stench of a burnt popcorn bag. People are sneezing. They sneezed during the spring and summer because of the pollen and the dusty weather. They will sneeze now because of the lack of air circulation.

Garden furniture and barbecues are not stored. They can be seen all over the cities – covered in four inches of snow – abandoned to the elements for six months of the year. Patio umbrellas are folded down, but not removed. All is still. Human life will not continue outdoors for another six months.

Within a day or two, snowmen begin to appear. They are basic shapes – some of them no more than amorphous blobs with damp and decaying sticks for arms and lumps of charcoal for eyes. After a week or two, the snowmen begin to look more accomplished, with carrots for noses, red scarves around their defined necks and woollen hats upon their rotund crowns. By early December, full-scale snow sculptures can be seen. Families construct snow families – exact replicas of themselves. Time is spent modelling features into the snow faces, until the snowmen look real enough to pass for an albino family holding a lawn party. Some families are better than others at making them. People will drive slowly by the house of a known snowman expert, wondering if this year's efforts could possibly outstrip last year's glory.

Minnesota now has a roof. The permanent snow clouds give the impression of being constantly indoors. The roof will not come off until spring.

At Hallowe'en, you walk cautiously, cocking an eye out for frozen puddles. By mid-November, small lakes have developed a thin layer of ice. The freeze is coming. By Christmas, all is frozen. The granddaddy of them all – Lake Superior – freezes over about one year in every three. The knowledge that the lake is about 40 square miles smaller than the island of Ireland only makes this fact even more impressive.

Nature adapts. Animals that cannot cope with the extreme change in weather sleep until it changes back. Bears have gorged themselves all summer long. Their last meals consisted primarily of hair and twigs in an attempt to block themselves up so that they will not have to get up in the middle of the night to try and find the bathroom. Animals that don't live so long simply lay their eggs in a warm spot and die. Birds migrate south – well, most of them do. Ducks are in the minority: they stay behind and swim in a perpetual circular relay that will last until the thaw, constantly keeping a section of their lake or river from freezing.

The snow seems to crash to the earth all around me – but I cannot hear a sound. I close the apartment windows, and ready myself for a season of stale air, cat hair and prime time TV. It is winter again in Minnesota.

***

On the day before the election, it is still too close to call. The snows have subsided for a day and torrential rain pours down on the cities. I brave the weather to go to the 8th Street Market to buy some emergency supplies – ice cream, potato chips and a frozen mozzarella and garlic pizza. A hooded figure comes charging towards me in the rain. He is wet.

"Hi – have you get a moment?"

"Sure – why not?" I have as much time as he needs – but no need to let him know that.

"Oh great – thanks for stopping. I've been out canvassing all day and you're the first person who's stopped to talk to me."

'Hmm – is this the time to tell him that I can't vote?'

"Basically, I stand for better schools, a fair deal for the elderly, a…"

"Er, can I stop you there? I won't be voting. I'm not allowed to do so legally. I'm only visiting here from Ireland."

"Oh. I see…" (silence) "Well, you take care now."

And off he goes. Pleasant enough chap – Ben Something-or-other is his name. He is only about my age – I kind of admired his determination. I go home and called a few friends, telling them to consider Ben Something-or-other in the election. They don't, and he doesn't win.

"Oh yeah – I know him," ventured one friend. "He's a jerk."

Soon, the big day arrives. I am excited – one of the few around who seemed to be. The polls are still too close to call. It is knife-edge stuff in Minnesota – a very unusual situation considering that the State *always* votes Democrat. In 1984, when Reagan pummelled Mondale in the Presidential election, Reagan won by forty-nine States to one. Guess which was the one.

The Democrats are trying everything they can to get the vote out around the Cities. Jesse Jackson led a prayer breakfast on the University campus. Tens of thousands of last-minute phone-calls are being made to undecided or apathetic voters. Local businesses are even doing their part. Chipotle, for example, is giving a free burrito to anyone who voted that day.

At around noon, Marie and a friend go to cast their votes. I tag along. The local polling station is in a church/community centre just off 8th Street SE – less than five minute's walk away. As it is not snowing, walking is a possibility. I look into the wardrobe, trying to decide what to wear. I end picking the same thing that I have worn each time I have gone out recently – everything I own. It is still freezing out there.

Soon, we arrive at the polling station. There is a queue, which is encouraging to see.

"I hope you're all voting for Nader – I'm gonna!" shouts a guy at the top of the line.

Another elderly gentleman comments that he'd never seen such a crowd at a polling station in all of his life. We reach the head of the queue. I grab a passing official and ask him if it is OK for me to be there. I could just imagine the headlines:

'Democrats Use Bearded Irishmen To Illegally Cast Votes', 'Irishman In Vote Scandal Shocker', and 'Bearded Irishman's Alien Lovechild Kidnapped'. Of course, the headlines all depended on the newspaper.

"Oh sure – you're more than welcome to look around. The American voting system comprises of an Electoral College. Minnesota has eleven votes – whichever candidate gets at least 50 per cent of these is elected. Here is the ballot – you fill it in – it gets fed into the machine…"

He goes on like this for another four or five minutes. He doesn't pause to take a single breath of air during the entire lecture. But I like him. He is a big fat jolly man – an enthusiastic one who just wants to help. He leaves me soon after – I think he overheard someone in the queue saying that they don't fully understand how the Electoral College system works. Last I heard, he is still there explaining it to her.

Now, in America, every civic office imaginable is on the ballot: President; State Senator; Congressman; Sanitation Commissioner; City Council; Judge. Everything. All are listed on a giant card, with ovals beside each name. If you want to vote for someone, you need only fill in the oval with pencil.

But there is more – something that I delighted in. In Ireland, and most of Europe, if you cannot decide whom to vote for, you have three choices: don't vote; vote for a randomly chosen candidate; or write an alternative name on the ballot – which will cause it to be thrown out as a 'Spoiled Vote'. However, in America, there is a specific section for a 'Write-in Candidate'. If you don't like the official choices, you can *legally* nominate another person of your choosing.

It is not my first appearance on a ballot, having been the humiliated and heavily defeated third-place candidate in the Maynooth Student Union Presidential Elections in 1999. In the 2000 American elections, I manage to garner one vote for the office of City Commissioner for the 4th District (courtesy of Marie) and one (courtesy of Marie's friend) for Soil and Water Commissioner for Conservation.

Wow! Not two months in the country and I have already convinced some citizens that I am good enough to run a small part of it! I wonder what the embassy would say? I am a proud man.

Marie hands her ballot to an election worker, who scans it into a voting machine. She gets an 'I Voted' sticker (necessary for the free Burrito). Her friend gets an 'I Voted' sticker. And I get an 'I Voted' sticker, which I've kept to this day. I don't let on. Nor do I complain that technically, I should have gotten an 'I've Been Voted For' sticker – I am happy enough.

We return home. I plonk myself down in front of the TV. It is a little after 1.00 p.m. I will still be there at nine o'clock the next morning. I am so nervous. Turnout is a little better than expected – but, although pundits are making their predictions, they really don't know who is going to win. Who indeed would be Minneapolis's next Soil and Water Commissioner for Conservation? Would I be elected?

***

Well, we all know what happened next. The election would be a double whammy for me, though. Not only is Al Gore not sworn in as the next President of the USA – despite the small, inconsequential fact that he *won* the election, but I garner too few votes to challenge for either the City Commissioner or Soil and Water Commissioner offices.

I never gave up hope that Al Gore would win. Deep down, I never believed that a man like George W. Bush would be sworn in as President. Even as he stood to take the oath of office the following January, I held out hope that somehow sense would prevail, and Al Gore would get the job.

I am genuinely worried at the prospect of Bush becoming President – especially if he turns environmental law over to business to regulate. My air quality, and therefore my health, would, in Ireland, be directly affected by this man's election. His attitude to employees – supporting low wages and outsourcing – is still worrying. He is setting a precedent that European governments could follow. He is not a 'good' man – never mind being a 'great' one. Yet he shrouds everything he does in mystery, claiming victories where he has lost, and talking in a pseudo-biblical language that makes religious people think that he's on their side – but he's not.

I wrote a very interesting piece on the election in my journal, dated '1 December'. I think that it's worth reading – even though I'm not entirely sure if I still agree with it or not:

> Great men and women are born every minute. Some will never be known for what they are due to when they are born, where they are born and the popularity or otherwise of the field in which their greatness lies.
>
> The Western world is dominated by the USA. They work to a capitalist model and feel that everyone else should too. They are big enough to impose this ideology and, as long as this continues, they can pretty much have dominance over the entire planet. It is thus that a great man – and I say 'man' as this world is not yet egalitarian – stands a great chance of being recognised if he is himself an American.
>
> There is, however, a problem – for just as great men and

women are born every minute, so too are fools. Many are great – but by noise rather than virtue. Many of these men and women rise to power (forgetting that lasting history is written by great men and women!)

What is happening today in 2000 in America is a mental civil war. The two main factions are well represented by both Al Gore – a man who bears all the hallmarks of greatness (in a public service sense – not a leadership one) and George W. Bush – a man who will have to reckon with great historians.

The reason for the impasse? Americans have been led to believe that all are born equal. If so, this makes all either great or stupid, by their own logic. The problem lies in the democratic hierarchy – unfortunately, fools have as much right to govern as do great men and, as all are born equal, a common neutral leader cannot be chosen.

Perhaps it's time to stop dispensing the lie that 'All are born equal', and replace it with the more truthful 'All are, equally, born.'

***

To say that music plays a big part in American life is an understatement, as is to say that it plays no part. Marie is an American. Americans like music. Therefore, Marie must like music. Brilliant.

This being the case, I decide to book a concert for her birthday – my first foray into the American music scene. Marie is a fan of the Indigo Girls. It just so happens that they are playing in the Cities around her birthday. Perfect. Two tickets please: 'The Indigo Girls Plus Support'. Great! Support! I loved them when I saw them play in Dublin last year. I ask for two of the best tickets they have left.

Turns out that the best tickets they have left are the only tickets they have left. We are seated just about as far from the stage as it is possible to be. We occupy the last two seats of the top row of the upper circle in the Orpheum Theatre. The Gods sit a couple of rows in front of us, getting their big bearded heads in the way for the entire performance.

A noise not dissimilar to clapping comes from beneath us – I am too far away to tell what it is. It could be a passing train or a hail shower. Better look at the stage, just in case it is the act. I ask Marie – who has been in the theatre before, where the stage is. Between the two of us, we spot it – about two stops away on a Greyhound, looking akin to a shoebox on its side – shoes removed, of course.

A flea appears on the shoebox stage. Another train rumbles by in the distance and ears detect a brief hail shower. The flea takes tiny microphone and begins to tell us about herself. Apparently she is no ordinary flea – she is a Native American flea, who sings songs about oppression. Interesting. I don't remember Support being like this last year. Maybe they have a different line up for this tour.

The flea has little in the way of talent. She sings songs that are essentially poorly written poetry with fancy words put to A Minor and G on an acoustic guitar. She sings a song about her son, Justice – his very name proving that there is none.

Soon, she finishes, apparently with rain dance music of some sort, as no sooner has she left the stage than the hail started again.

Next up is a creature that looks to be bigger than a flea – a fly, perhaps? The fly, it turns out, is David Crosby and his acoustic guitar. I turn to Marie to see if she enjoyed it too. Her scowl tells me that she did not.

"He's as old as my dad. Why would I pay to see my dad on stage?"

I am about to tell her that she is missing the point – that David Crosby is a timeless artist whose age is meaningless and whose music is still fresh. At that point, David himself begins to speak.

"My God – I am so old. I've been singing these songs for so long."

Marie's scowl becomes practically vitriolic.

It is now 10.00 p.m. Odd that the Indigo Girls have not yet taken to the stage. The theatre is in an urban area that I imagine would have to close by 11.00 p.m. I see some movement on the stage, and another insect of some description comes into view. Just one? Maybe I read the tickets wrong and we have actually come to see the Indigo Girl.

Nope. It is not even a musical act. It is Winona LaDuke, naturally enough, the Green Party Vice-Presidential candidate. She proceeds to give a long speech that brings more hail and passing trains. This is very odd. The concert is now due to end in less than forty-five minutes. We have not seen the Indigo Girls. And we have heard a lot of speeches about righteousness. A very odd concert indeed.

Suddenly, the Indigo Girls are on stage, and giving it welly. But only for one song. They stop to give a speech of their own. Then they give it socks for another five minutes…before stopping to give another speech. All in all, the Indigo Girls are on stage for a mere half-hour – and play only four songs! And the strangest thing – they get a standing ovation.

It is only a year later when we see them in Dublin that I realise what I had seen. They took to the stage in Dublin and began to sing away. It was good stuff. They then stopped to make a speech about some female soldiers that they encountered in Central America.

"We thought they were cool," they told the audience.

The audience laughed.

They sang another song, and stopped again to give a little speech. In the middle of it, an Indigo Girl looked out into the audience.

"Why are you all laughing?"

They held a little conference amongst themselves, and didn't give another speech for the rest of the concert.

What I saw in America is a classic case of playing to the audience. Some go for the music. Some go for the political views that the band hold. Both get what they are looking for. When they came to Ireland, they didn't realise that audience interaction should only be kept to saying how great Dublin is, etc. They hadn't realised that people had come to hear the music, and the music only.

Marie, incidentally, is very annoyed with the concert in Minneapolis – she came to hear them play.

What this little story highlights is the fact that music is very highly politicised in America – if not all over the world. A concert is an expression and a celebration of a particular idea or lifestyle. A 'Country and Western' concert is a celebration of core rural values and working class lifestyle. 'Rock and Roll' is still a celebration of life. Even after it had been stripped bare of dignity and justice in the slums of New Orleans and other cities in the South, rock and roll showed that it could never be stripped of soul. In this vein, an Indigo Girls concert is a venue to discuss social injustice.

America is home to many different types of music. The songs tell of heroes, heroines, ideals, injustices. American music – the type that started with cowboys and hobos, represents the first great departure in popular music in recent centuries – it gives the people the chance to be recognised. It is not necessary to be rich or famous to be celebrated in an American song. It is a very democratic type of music – one that could really only have begun in America, with its heritage of an America Dream – where every dog has his day. Woodie Guthrie sang about a land that 'belongs to you and me'. Johnny Cash sang about Ira Hayes [who raised the Stars and Stripes on Iwo Jima], showing how even those who have been marginalised still make important contributions to society. Twentieth century music is a celebration of the triumph of the free spirit that is undeniably found in the idea of America. As a man from a country with an extensive musical heritage, I find this refreshing, as the Irish music I grew up with spoke only about one of two subjects: either 'suffering' or 'unattainable women'.

And looking at it from this angle, I finally have an understanding for those damn 'Pop Idol' shows that plague America, where they scour the nation looking for people who sing – even if most of the singers do so without any soul. It follows on from the idea that music belongs to 'the people', and can be sung by the people it has been written about. It also goes some way to bringing about an understanding of the 'problem' of sharing music over the internet. If music is truly written by the people and for the people, then exactly how much power should the large corporations who merely control distribution wield?

I am still trying to figure out what my musical tastes are. I grew up listening alternately to Metallica and Al Jolson, with a little Nirvana thrown in for good measure. In short, my musical tastes are…unrefined. It is not until later that I discover the music and the meaning of artists such as Johnny Cash and Tom Waits. Being in America really helps me to branch out. American music shops sell much of the same titles that are sold back home, but there is a difference. There are huge local sections. There are acts that have made it here that have not yet reached Europe. Back home, I grew up with music shops that sold the best of whatever is in the UK charts and the few albums that are considered 'classics'. Here, I find choice. I find artists that are not global superstars, but musicians. And I am arrogant enough not to immediately realise what I have discovered. I continue to turn my nose up at these artists – artists that obviously aren't good enough to make it worldwide. I completely miss the point. The penny only drops when I hear the music played in other places – friends' houses, car radios, even airports. I find myself tapping my foot along. Then I find myself humming the tune. I am unable to sleep that night – the music swirling around my brain. I have to buy it. And, when I do, I usually realise that the hummed song has morphed into something unrecognisable while in brain storage. I end up hating the track, but loving everything else about the album.

Music is alive and well in America – no matter what *American Idol* may make you think.

***

It is coming to the end of my stay. I have to think about leaving Marie – although it will only be for a couple of weeks. She'll then come to Ireland to live with me. I have to think about gifts too. When my brother and I were are kids, an uncle would always give us a gift of some of the local currency of the country he had most recently visited. We loved it, and were always fascinated by it. That's what I will do.

I have no credit card and no bank account here in America. What I do have is a big pile of Traveller's Cheques. Being an unemployed…well, not student…not really traveller either…Being unemployed means that I don't have any money coming in. I am totally reliant on any monies that I brought with me. This means that after rent and bills, I am left with only about $80 a week. It isn't much – but it is enough to do nothing on.

I divide my Traveller's Cheques up into batches. I will cash in about $100 each week. I hide the batches in a money pouch which I then hide under the crate of the fat cat that lives in the apartment. And if the cat's owner happens to be reading this – I know that you don't necessarily think that your cat is fat – but she does have an awful lot of excess skin.

I am not worried about the cat getting at my cheques. I know that she is too inactive an animal to actually destroy them. The cheques also have my passport number on them – which means that she can't cash them at any rate.

Now, I'm a demon when it comes to spending money. I don't know what I spend it on, but I usually do have a lot of nothing to prove that I spent it. My family compare me to Jack and his 'magic beans'. Knowing that I have no financial back-up, I want to take extra caution with the cheques. This is why I decided to make a weekly trip to the bank rather than cash them all in at once.

Not every America bank deals with foreign currency or Traveller's Cheques. In fact, such banks are a rarity in the Twin Cities. I manage to locate one bank in Dinkytown that will be able to accommodate me. Every week I walk (freezing) to the bank. Every week I hand in my cheque and passport. Every week they comment on me being Irish – a fact I am only too well aware of. Every week they pressure me into opening an account. Every week I refuse, knowing that it is probably technically illegal for me to do so.

With money in my pockets, the world will briefly be my oyster, and I its pearl. I buy rubbish – much to Marie's disapproval: Jesse Ventura key rings; a joke guide to Voodoo, complete with practice doll; a deck of playing cards depicting the great lighthouses of North America (Marie hates lighthouses. I think it will be funny to buy it for her – but I forget why it is that I think that). In a word, crap.

Knowing that I will need about $20 to 'buy' gifts, I curtail my crap purchasing indulgences for a week. While in the States, a new Dollar coin is launched, depicting the Shoshone guide Sacagawea, who had aided the explorers Lewis and Clarke. Grand. I'll get me some of them. I also read that there is a $2 bill. It is rare enough to come by it during everyday spending, but they could be gotten easily from the bank. Gotta get me some of them too.

I have a problem, however. I am far too embarrassed to go up to a bank teller (after all, they all know me) and ask for a 'twenty' to be changed into five $2 bills and a roll of Sacagaweas. But surely Marie wouldn't be. After all, she is an American – a local. I get her to do it by using the ol' 'If you love me you'll do it' ruse, which I think a better ploy than using the Voodoo doll, or threatening to sit the obese apartment feline on her face as she sleeps if she doesn't. Marie agrees to do it, but has quite literally held it against me ever since.

I stand by the door as Marie approaches the teller. She places a $20 bill on the counter.

"Hi – I'd like to change this…for a roll of Sacagawea Dollars and five twos."

"What?"

"I'd like to change this for a roll of Sacagawea Dollars and five twos."

She is, by now, both embarrassed, and hating me. What I am essentially doing is trading one woman – Marie – for another – Sacagawea. Either way – whichever I end up with – I ain't getting no lovin' tonight.

There is a bit more banter that I do not catch between Marie and the teller. Then there is some banter that I *do* catch.

Marie turns to look at me, and speaks to the teller (who is, for the purposes of this sentence, the tellee):

"They're for my Irish boyfriend – he wants them as a gift."

'Bollox. She's sold me out.'

Now I look worse than I would have if I had gone up to get them myself. I look like a fool, standing at the bank door, looking intently at the transaction, having sent my girlfriend up to the counter to do some ridiculous dirty work. Jesse James once famously held up a bank in Northfield, Minnesota, as he did all over the United States. James escaped capture, but this was the last bank he ever attempted to rob. Now I know how he must have felt to get caught.

In the end, I get my money – but the costs have been greater than $20. When I return home, I give the money as a gift to a few people. They all look at me like I have ten heads and horns. Except for my brother. Turns out that my brother and I are the only ones who found getting money as a gift to be legitimate.

Everyone except for my brother!

CHAPTER FIVE

Jaywalking in St Paul

My final week has arrived. It is coming into mid-December, and I am getting ready to leave America. I do all of those things one leaves until the last minute – suitcase packing, eating the mysterious jars of food-type substances that have been lurking at the back of the press since the first week (turned out to be pumpkin mix)…and developing photos.

I had graduated from University the week before departing from Ireland. I had brought photos to show Marie. In them, I look well. I have short, tight hair. I have a neatly trimmed beard. I look happy and stress-free. Although not thin by any stretch of the imagination, I look well – the little weight I tend to always carry suited me quite well, made me look healthy.

Marie picks up the photos taken during my stay. They have been taken over the course of the past month or so. I open them. I can't believe my eyes. What have I become? It seems that months of professional and social inactivity have taken its toll: I have reverted to a feral state. In the first photo, I am wearing not clothes, but cloth – bed sheets. I have taken to wandering around the apartment during these past months as it is too cold to wander outside, wearing either bed sheets or – as the next picture will reveal in a most disturbing manner – a white silk ladies' kimono/dressing gown with a floral pattern and navy trim.

Sounds pretty bad – doesn't it? Then, I look at my face in the picture. It is haggard. I have not had a haircut since the one I got for my graduation – and would not have another until the week after arriving back in Ireland. Also, I have not been looking after my beard properly. To use an analogy from the movie *Gladiator*, my beard is now more ageing emperor than dashing gladiator. My cheeks are carrying false weight. They are puffy and unnatural. And then there are my eyes. Bagged. Black.

During late puberty, my wisdom teeth held a conference and voted unanimously to opt for the painful way forward. Slowly, they scraped their way through the jaw, through the gums. I never went to a dentist to get them removed. For anyone who hasn't experienced this 'free-range wisdom teeth' option, let me briefly explain. The teeth begin to move from deep within the jawbone. They hurt immensely at this stage. Then, they meet the gums, where they carve them into a lattice. The gums surrounding swell just enough that one bites – or rather crunches – them at least once a day. And all the time, there is pain – a dull, beating pain that has a stronger life force than myself. If you've ever heard a constant note played really, really low on a cello – so low that it sounds more sinister than musical – you'll begin to have an idea as to what it feels like. The pain lives for a week here, a month there. From the age of seventeen it paid me regular visits. Then, from the age of twenty or so, it stopped. I was so glad that it was finished...or was it?

The day – the very day – I arrived in the USA, my wisdom teeth started again. The pain did not stop, oddly enough, until the day I arrived back in Ireland. I spent my months in America suffering a constant cello-playing dull pain. I could see it in my eyes in the photographs – it had taken its toll. It quite literally drove me to despair on more than one occasion. The fact that I had nothing much to do in America, coupled with the fact that it was too cold to do *anything*, meant that I had plenty of time to wallow in the pain. That's why I ended up staying in bed until mid-day. That's why I climbed into a comfortable kimono and stayed there for months. That's why I got to know Ricki Lake and Jerry Springer on what seemed to be personal terms.

The other people in the apartment worked all day – Marie included. That meant that on days when there was nothing to do, I would stay in the apartment by myself, curled up on the couch and pumped full of painkillers to dull a dull pain, wearing a kimono, and, most bizarre of all, with the fat apartment cat assuming her favourite position – draped across my shoulders like a fur.

In recent months, it has come to my attention that certain painkillers may cause heart trouble. What if I had a heart attack while everyone is at work? Imagine being found like that – cat, kimono and all? I'm surprised that I hadn't realised this – it was, after all, during my morbid 'Say something witty or intelligent before you go to sleep in case you die during the night and they turn out to be your last words' phase.

Here lies Seán who was found dead wearing nothing but bed sheets and a live cat.
I don't think it would matter much what my last words were in this case.

It is ironic. I have felt like an outsider during my entire stay – due in no small part to the fact that the Immigration official at the airport had put the fear of God into me. Now that my final week has arrived, I finally feel that I have learned enough about America to participate. I finally feel that I can have an opinion on things rather than merely accepting them as they are because I am an outsider. The daily news broadcasts finally have meaning for me. A gunman on the run to the south of the Cities. I was there not two weeks ago. A car chase in Hinckley. I've eaten there! A robbery in Dinkytown. I live there!

The story that I finally choose to pluck up the courage to participate with is a low-key one. In hindsight, it was a poor choice. On the news one night, as they talk exclusively about places I know, they report on the introduction of a jaywalking ban in downtown St Paul. Not a big story, I know.

Marie arrives home from work. Greeting me as she removes her coat – sorry, coats – she asks how my day was. Apparently the fact that I am dressed in a bed sheet and wearing a cat has given nothing away.

"They've passed a law against jaywalking in downtown St Paul."

"Oh…I see. What do you want for dinner?"

Obviously I am not selling it correctly.

"So…what do you think they'd do if they caught you?"

"I dunno. Will we send out for pizza?"

OK – maybe it is too overwhelming a story for her to process. I'll try again later. At that moment, the door opens again, and the guy who shares the apartment walks in. Taking his jacket off, he greets us and asks how our day went – again, obviously taking my appearance for granted.

"Fine. Do you want to order out for pizza with us?" asks Marie.

"They've outlawed jaywalking in St Paul."

"Sure. Pizza would be nice."

What is with these people? I give them gold – an insight to their…nay, *our* world – and I get nothing. Not a peep. Do they not realise what this will mean? The act of walking across the street could have them branded 'outlaws'. The street is no longer a safe place for feet. 'The Street Is Not For Feet!'

That evening, after dinner, I decide to call home and arrange for my parents to pick me up from the airport when my plane gets into Dublin in a week's time.

"Why are you calling now? There's still a week to go!" says Marie.

But the phone is already ringing at the other end. I am sorry – they just have to know.

"Hello Dad? Seán here. Yeah – I'm going to be back in Dublin at 9.00 a.m. on Tuesday morning. How's things here? They've outlawed jaywalking in St Paul. The weather? But…yes. The weather is cold."

Another battle lost. That evening, I resign myself to defeat on the issue. I chose a poor issue with which to begin my contribution to American society. I picked an issue that nobody cared about. Why? Everyone drives in the Cities. It has no more relevance to them than the law that states it is illegal to enter the State of Wisconsin from Minnesota while wearing a duck on your head. I kid you not. There's also an antiquated State law that requires people to tip their hats to cows! A swing and a miss.

Over dinner – an excellent Papa John's pizza and a bottle of root beer – we talk about my leaving and what we will do during our last week. The day before my flight will be Marie's graduation. We'll go to that. It also means that Marie is finally finished with her studies – and we can spend a couple of days together.

We decide to do some of the touristy things on Saturday. We'll do the Science Museum and the State Capitol. The State Capitol?! That is in…St Paul. Realising this, I impart a valuable piece of advice to Marie: We had better be careful about how we cross the street on Saturday – Jaywalking is now illegal in St Paul.

***

That Saturday, we take the bus to St Paul. It travels though some of the poorer areas of the Cities – Frogtown and Midway amongst them. Soon, the bus drops us off – right by the State Capitol. It is an impressive structure – a white, domed building in a Classical style. It is not yet a hundred years old. Inside, it is magnificent. Beautiful, but not overpowering. The words of famous thinkers are etched into the walls – including Daniel O'Connell from Ireland, the great Emancipator.

A guest book lies open on top of a pedestal by an information booth. I sign it.

"Would you like to add a flag to our map?" asks an assistant.

The idea is a nice one – a world map into which the visitor can stick a flag representing their home country. But there is a difference – it is a map like no other I have ever seen. This map depicts the Americas in the centre. To the right of them, Europe, Africa and Asia as far as the Caspian Sea. To the left, Australia and the rest of Asia. It looks so very strange to me – an unusual degree of effort to express the belief that America is the centre of the planet. Why can't maps be like they are back home? And then I have a thought. Do maps back home depict Europe in the centre for the same reason?

"You're from Ireland: sorry – no green flags!"

"Not to worry. I'll take a blue – the colour of the Kings of Tara."

Not having a clue what I am talking about, she tells me that she has only red left.

"Not to worry – the colour of the Craobh Ruadh." [The Red Branch Knights.]

Smiling, confused, she hands me a red flag. Patriotically, I stab Ireland in the area that its kidneys would be, if for some reason it came to life.

Following this, we get a tour of the Capitol, including the office of Jesse Ventura. I like Jesse – even though he had recently been in trouble for blaming the lack of a complete street grid system in St Paul on the fact that it was built by drunken Irish. I – and everyone I talk to back home – think it is a pretty funny remark. Jesse is not in that day, and I would not get to meet him.

It is a very pleasant tour, and there is a lot to see there as it houses not only the Governor's office, but also the State Supreme Court, the State Senate and the State House of Representatives. When the tour is over, we go to the German-themed cellar restaurant for lunch, and leave to brave the freezing cold by walking to the Science Museum.

The snow is falling. Actually, since there is more than one snowflake, it should read: snow is falling. A dry breeze is whispering into our faces, cracking them dry of any moisture. The air is clear. The ground is frozen. Within five minutes – despite wearing all I own, including two pairs of winter socks split evenly between my two feet – my toes are numb, my ears are red and screaming, my nose is unaware of the fact that it is running and my (by now impressive) beard has begun to frost over. The ground is slippery – we watch our every step.

Soon, we reach downtown St Paul, walking past the stadium of the newly incorporated Ice Hockey team, Minnesota Wild. The Science Museum is just a few short blocks away.

St Paul is a little more foreboding than Minneapolis, a little darker and a little less welcoming. It too has suffered greatly as a functioning downtown since the construction of the Mall of America. It has a colourful enough history. It is called St Paul after the first church that was built in the area. And that's pretty much the story you'll find in a lot of the tour guides. A few of them, though, tell the true story. St Paul was originally called Pig's Eye, after the proprietor of one of the first bars in the area. The idea of being named after a bar owner's bestial nickname just didn't appeal to the growing population. I think that re-naming the town after a church, in the minds of the townspeople, brought them a little closer to God.

We are standing at a junction. We needed to cross it in order to make it to the Museum. But there is a problem – although Marie doesn't see it. There is no cross walk. The only way to get across is...to jaywalk! And what is parked at the traffic lights to our right? A police car.

"Marie – we can't cross here. It's illegal to jaywalk in St Paul."

"What – since when?" asks Marie, as she strides out into the middle of the road.

I remain calm. I know that this is not the time to panic. There are two reasons for this. First of all, being panicky would mean that I am more likely to crack under the pressure of interrogation when they haul me in for being an outlaw. Second of all, if I panic, I sweat. If I sweat, there will be more things to freeze.

Out I step – one eye on my destination, the other on the cops. I have no doubt that the embassy have, by now, given them my photo. Being arrested for a heinous crime is a sure way to get me deported, if I am lucky, or on the special Greyhound to Sandstone if I am not. I quickly catch up with Marie, who is moving quite fast – or, as the locals say, 'bookin' it' across the road. The police car does not move. No doubt they are calling for back up.

We have, by now, reached half-way: three lanes down, three to go. We stop to let a car pass. Well, actually, we stop to prevent a car from hitting the jaywalkers. 'Stopping' is not what we need. Marie remains calm throughout the whole affair. I admire her complete disdain for the rules, and feel worried by her obviously complete disdain for me. Four lanes. No cops. Five lanes. They still haven't moved. Six lanes. We've made it.

"Well, here's the Science Museum."

Science Museum? Is she serious? That is old news. Now, we have to think of our survival. We already have a 40-metre head start on the cops. I don't want to stop these legs until they reach either Mexico or, more preferably given its relative proximity to the Cities, Canada.

I take a quick look back. The cop car is still there...and there are at least four other jaywalkers crossing at the junction. Phew! Maybe the cops didn't see the news report I saw. But that doesn't matter. Caught or not, convicted or not, I know the truth in my heart. I am an outlaw, and nothing can ever change that.

***

The following day I attend Marie's graduation. Like me, she now holds a degree in Anthropology, and is fighting off the advances of major employers. The graduation itself is a nice enough ceremony. It is a much, much bigger affair than mine had been. It involves grandiose music, sung by classically trained singers. It involves a full-scale brass band. Mr Davidow, the Ambassador to Mexico gives a truly forgettable speech about how America's Cold War-winning capitalist model is the envy of the world, whether or not the world knows it. As graduates, it would be their job to remind the world of this fact. The graduates are called up and presented with their degrees. Or, at least, with the holders for their degrees. It seems that the graduates have technically not yet graduated, as they still have to receive confirmation of a passing grade. The actual presentation of the degree parchment would not be as big an affair as that for the holders. Rather, it will involve a ceremony consisting of the Master of the Post ritually pushing the parchment into the Letter Box of Destiny.

The graduation is held in Northrop Hall on campus. It is a very, very unusual building. The entire structure is actually a huge pipe organ – the pipes set into the walls, running above the ceiling. But best of all, the conservation committee for Northrop is called 'The Friends of the Northrop Organ'. Good stuff.

The following day is my last full day in America. We have a quiet day followed by a pleasant evening out at a good Mexican restaurant called La Cucaracha. At least that's what I think it is called – I could have been reading a health notice saying that the restaurant is 'con Cucarachas' ('infested with cockroaches'). The food is quite good – even if it is…less than authentic. Minnesota is more or less completely settled by Swedes. Swedish food is quite nice – but it is at the opposite end of the spice scale to Mexican. Thus, most Minnesotan Mexican food has been tailored to suit the local palate. 'Spicy' does not exist. I actually know Minnesotans who will not eat bell peppers or red onions because they consider them too spicy. It is a little surprising on one level, that spicy foods are not more popular, given the excessive cold that the State has to endure.

I go to bed that night aware that my American odyssey is about to come to an end. It is stuffy in the bedroom, but we cannot open the window. The outside temperature is -30°C.

***

The plan for the next morning is to hang out with Marie until she has to go to work. She gets up early and cooks me a breakfast of vegetarian corn dogs (which are surprisingly good) and, with the help of a certain black woman with a perpetual grin, pancakes. I decide to dress for breakfast. I would never again wear the kimono or bed sheet. Although I've since looked for a replacement bed sheet, I've never quite managed to find one in my size.

At 10.45 a.m., I walk Marie to the bus stop. She has to go to work – only three weeks until she joins me in Dublin. She'll need the cash. It is cold outside. The news put it at what I work out to be -27°C. She steps onto the bus and is gone.

I trudge back to the apartment. A friend will collect me in a little over an hour, to bring me to the airport. I will get there before noon and have almost four hours to wait – but I can't say 'no' to a lift and have to walk for twenty-five freezing minutes to the bus-stop.

An hour. Just enough time to pack. My suitcase is already full of useless and unused clothes that I brought from Ireland. T-shirts. Five of them. What was I thinking? Light, cloth runners – or 'Tennies', as sports shoes are known in America. Another good choice. Step in a puddle and they freeze. My coat – an ordinary brown jacket that I bought last winter to deal with the Irish cold. When I first showed it to Marie, she laughed. I ended up wearing her winter coat from when she was a teenager for the duration of my stay.

Then there is the crap I have accumulated over the past few months. My 'Al Gore For President' sign that has hung on a wall in every place I've since lived. My collection of newspapers from the election. My 'Al Gore – 43rd President of the United States' silver coin from the Franklin Mint. Hmm…I am starting to see a pattern.

I pack the gifts. I decide that although bringing money as a gift is the greatest idea a man ever had, it might not be enough. I buy some local delicacies for people back home to try. Candy Corn (left over from Hallowe'en). Tootsie Rolls. Hershey's Chocolate. I am going to be so popular – so long, that is, as nobody eats the candy.

When packed, I walk to the living room. I have a half-hour to wait. The fat cat is perched on the back of the sofa, looking at me in the same way she always has. Is she puzzled by me? Afraid of me? Amazed by me? Afraid that I am going to eat her? Wondering how she can eat me? I never figure it out. I play with her a little. Then it is time to go.

U2 is on the CD player when I get into the car. There is not much conversation. What do you say when you've already wished someone goodbye? Traffic is light – we are between rush hours. Twenty minutes later, we pulled in at the Lindbergh Terminal. We hug goodbye.

I enter the airport and look for the Continental desk. Might as well check in early and have the freedom to walk around the airport without my luggage. Four hours. What the hell am I and my remaining $10 going to do for four hours?

I approach the desk – no one in the queue.

"Hi – I know I'm early – but can I check in now?"

"Newark? You're going to Newark? Honey, there's a big, big storm coming – your flight's been cancelled."

Oh great.

"Look – the last flight that will be able to go to Newark today is leaving in fifteen minutes. I can switch you to that if you want. It's not guaranteed that it will make it – it might have to turn around."

"I'll take it."

Time to run, Forrest, run.

Up to the airport x-ray machine with my guitar. No one there so I run through. Onto the moving floor.

"Excuse me. Pardon me. Sorry. Can I squeeze by there?"

To the gate.

"Has this flight left?"

"No – but you'd better run down to it. I'll call them to let them know you're coming."

On to the plane. Made it. 12.10 p.m. I find my seat. Or, rather, I find my seats. The flight is only half full. The air hostesses give a lightning quick safety presentation. Before they have finished, the airplane is sitting on the runway about to take off. And *whoosh*.

"This is your Captain speaking. We're gonna try to shave a little off the flight time, to see if we can make Newark before the storm. This unfortunately means that we don't have an in-flight meal for you – we don't have the time to take one on board. I'll talk to you a little later when we reach our cruising altitude."

Great. A four-hour flight and no food. One of the stewardesses finds a box of peanuts and begins doling them out. At least they are trying – and trying pretty hard, too. After all, they are putting themselves out, as far as I am concerned, to get me to my connecting flight.

Let me see. A four-hour flight…We'll be in Newark a little after 4.00 p.m. Minnesota time. That will give me about five hours to arse around the airport. Why am I still on Minnesota time? I take my watch from my wrist and set it to Newark time – one hour forward. I haven't got a lot of cash on me. I could always break into the five twos and ten Sacagaweas. I also have Tootsie Rolls and Candy Corn.

There is an announcement. Continental have decided to take the blame for the weather, and give us all $25 of vouchers to spend on whatever we want in Newark Airport. I'll fly with them again. As a stewardess comes through the craft to issue the vouchers, I put my seat back and look out the window at the continent below.

About an hour into the flight, the Captain makes another

announcement to the passengers.

"Ladies and gentlemen, this is your Captain speaking. We've managed to pick up a little time and will be landing in Newark in just under an hour's time."

What! How in God's name have they managed to cut the flight time in half?

"It looks like we'll just miss the storm but will probably hit a little turbulence, so from here on in I'm turning on the 'Fasten Seatbelt' sign."

We don't hit a little turbulence that day. Nor would we narrowly miss the storm. Instead, we comfortably fly smack bang into the middle of it. Although I can't see them, I am sure that King Kong and Godzilla have grabbed hold of the craft and are shaking it around in anger. The stewardesses – strapped into their seats – are looking worried. There is tension and nervousness in the craft.

I am not really frightened, however. I figure that Continental would probably not want to risk the bad publicity that air crashes tend to bring. If they have decided that it is safe to fly, then it is safe to fly. It is even a little thrilling – very like being on a roller coaster, where the body is constantly perplexed at not being able to fix its centre of gravity.

We descend through the cloud barrier. Below us is the East Coast. Soon, we are flying over Manhattan. I can see the Statue of Liberty. I can see the buildings that make up the famous New York skyline. I can see the Washington Bridge. I can see the Twin Towers. It is really beautiful.

The airplane bumps its way down from air corridor to air corridor. The gales outside are raging. We get lower, and lower. Soon, we are at runway level – and have still not steadied. Then, with supreme professionalism, the craft steadies for less than a moment, and the plane touches down. I have made it. I now have more than six hours to kill in Newark Airport before my flight to Dublin. And I have $35 to spend.

I decide that this will be a good opportunity to eat all the things that I never plucked up the courage to try. I visit several fast food outlets and get a take-out in each one. I buy a Philly Cheese Steak and, although delicious, it must have had a different blood type to me, because my body rejected it. I buy a Cinnabon – which I had before and enjoyed, but it has been a while. I buy a Big Mac – which, incidentally, is the last time I ate at McDonalds. I buy a small slice of Chicago Pizza with a mysterious spiced flesh substance. I buy an excellent Coney Hot Dog. And I buy a Dr Pepper to wash it all down.

I am, by now, feeling ill. I have eaten far too much – but I suppose when in Rome…I make my way to the gate. Four hours left. I go to a newsstand and buy a *Time* magazine. There are TV sets all over the airport switched to CNN. The sad news of the day is that it now looks 99.9 per cent certain that Al Gore will not be the next President. The Supreme Court has issued a bizarre ruling that states, as far as I can make out, that it would be wrong to conduct a manual recount of the ballots in Florida because if Bush loses it, it will undermine his legitimacy as President. Damn right! What has just happened here?

By now, I have only a couple of bucks left. By the way – the phrase 'Bucks' comes from the fact that deerskins sold in the mid-19th century for about a dollar. Buck = Dollar. (Maybe I can get this book sold in the educational section.)

I look around. The seats around me are occupied by about twenty or so blonde girls all wearing 'Hooters' jackets. Turns out that they are not waiting to go to Ireland and are waiting on a flight at another nearby gate. They will go elsewhere to 'hoot' today.

After they leave, the place fills up with Irish. It is all too familiar.

"You can't get a decent cup of tea in New York."

"Isn't the food terrible? Can't get corned beef and cabbage anywhere."

"Ah Jasus – Mary. Didn't know you are in New York. Haven't seen you in years."

Although my flight has not yet left, I am already home.

***

A flight from America – anywhere in America – to Ireland is hell for one main reason. The flights tend to touch down between 7.00 a.m. and 9.00 a.m. As it is impossible to sleep on flights, that means trying to stay awake for at least another twelve hours to beat the jet lag.

My flight is due to land a little after 9.00 a.m. We touch down in Dublin Airport right on schedule, and taxi to the Terminal. We are due to exit via jetway – one of those movable corridors that connect the passengers right into the Terminal. But there is a problem. The jetway doesn't work and won't connect to the door. We are left inside the craft for another half-hour while they try to figure it out.

Now, usually I find this kind of thing funny, and laugh it off. However, this is the second time something like this has happened me in Dublin Airport. The previous year, when I arrived home after six months studying in Germany, there was no jetway for our airplane. Instead, they were to supply a staircase. Fair enough. However, when we touched down, there was no staircase there to meet us. Twenty minutes later one arrived – but it was for a different-sized aircraft and couldn't be used. A highly irate Captain kept us up-to-date – obviously as frustrated and bemused as his passengers. All in all, we had to wait an hour for the stairs to arrive.

I step onto the now-working jetway. I collect my bags and go to the Terminal, where my family wait for me. How will they greet me, I wonder? I am looking forward to seeing my parents and brother, 'Templeton le Fleur' again. They'll be overjoyed. We'll hug. All will be well.

Turns out that that's not exactly what happens. As I enter the meeting area, they are there to meet me. They do not say 'Seán – great to have you back'. They do not say, 'Seán – we've missed you'. I'd even have settled for 'Seán', followed by a handshake. In the end, I don't even get a 'Seán'.

"Hello – nice to see you all!"

"You smell like an arse. Doesn't he smell like an arse?"

(Sniff sniff)

"He does smell like an arse. Templeton – smell your brother. He smells like an arse."

(Sniff sniff)

"Why do you smell like an arse?"

I remind them that I have been travelling for a day, and that rather than rectal odour, they are probably experiencing a tired-body smell.

"Well, you still smell like an arse."

We walk to the car, and drive home. I have already begun pushing most of my American memories to the back of my mind. I don't know what else to do with them. What will I say when people ask me about my stay? I dressed in bed sheets and watched my beard freeze over? What did I make of America? What did I discover about the people who lived there? I honestly don't know, and it will take me years of contemplation to figure it all out. What I do know, however, is that my old friend 'Jet Lag' has returned. Quite frankly, I rather smell like an arse.

CHAPTER SIX

Home

Back in Ireland, I begin the arduous task of securing employment. I try my hand at a few different things. First, I try retail management in a souvenir store in Dublin city centre. I hate it and, by all accounts, the management hates me. Neither they nor I know quite how I ended up there. I don't have the required grit to succeed. All day long, I stock shelves full of tacky leprechauns and miniature Guinness bottles, while having my brain porridged as it listens to Irish music CDs played over and over and over again.

I do learn more about America, however. I discover more about the American image of Ireland. I discover the tricks the Irish have to turn to earn the appreciation of the dollar. Americans come to Ireland looking for a nation of cottiers and turf cutters. Instead they find a first world nation not dissimilar to theirs. The Ireland they seek – and, it must be said, the Ireland that they have been promised by Irish tourist authorities – exists mainly in souvenir shops. They come with an idea that they never realise – but the souvenirs tell otherwise.

In many ways, the tourist industry that has grown up in Ireland is an American industry. The model that the Irish have used is strikingly similar to that used by Disney and other American corporate icons – sell 'ideas', even if they don't reflect the reality.

A few months later, I land a job as a tour guide. I absolutely love the job, but the wages are poor. It's the kind of job that leaves me poorer on payday than beforehand. I bring busloads of Americans on city tours and tours to areas in the Irish countryside. In Dublin, I tell stories of corruption, prostitution, idiocy – and they love it. Those expecting a Disney Dublin are never disappointed – I give them something better than that. I give them a Dublin with which they can empathise. In Glendalough, a 6th-century monastic site, I give them anything but the reverence they expect from the site. This is something that I feel is important, as many Americans have difficulty understanding items of historical importance older than a few centuries, due to the relative youth of European-America and its culture. I tell them stories about people. The places began to make sense. Only in the Boyne Valley – an ancient settlement older than the pyramids – do I change the script. Nobody has a clue about the people that lived there, and so nothing concrete can either be told or ridiculed. So I sell the mystery of the place, and they lap it up.

My season working as a tour guide really helps me to understand the thought processes of Americans – about how what they want and expect to hear are not necessarily the same thing; about how to construct a neatly packaged story for them, to bring an historical site to life. And, most importantly, about the American need to belong and how to weave a story around them and their expectations.

One of the biggest Irish tourist industries is that of genealogy. America is one of its biggest customers. Many come looking for an ancestor, an address, a story that connects them to a place with deeper roots than America. It provides them with a sense of belonging to a people that are portrayed in American eyes as an oppressed and poor cousin. They will not only find roots – they will also find a sense of satisfaction as they fill the role of the emigrant done good. It is a need for a sense of belonging that I can understand and appreciate in 'Celtic Tiger' Ireland.

My next job is to prove a very interesting learning experience about America. In September, I am hired by the accounting firm of Arthur Andersen.

***

I wake, ready and eager for my first day in work. I am to start out doing general, background office work. I won't need a suit per se, but a shirt and tie are a must. I've always tried to live up to Oscar Wilde's idea that one should either be a work of art or wear a work of art. That being the case, I had spent the week beforehand shopping for a snappy tie. The tie I settle on is black and grey with depictions of New York scenes – the Statue of Liberty, the Empire State Building etc. Looking in the bathroom mirror, I knot the tie. The Twin Towers are the most prominent feature, pictured just below the knot.

I walk to work – my new flat is a mere twenty-minute walk from the City Centre and my new job. It is a grey day – typical for early autumn. Not too cold, though, which is always nice.

At nine, I arrive. I meet with my new boss – who has a cup of coffee ready for me. Smiling to hide the tears, I drink the only cup of coffee I have ever had in my entire life, as he talks to me about the position.

He leads me into the room I will be working in, and introduces me to the others. I begin working and the morning passes quietly.

Then, just before lunch, I hear on the radio that there has been an accident in Manhattan – an airplane has crashed into one of the Twin Towers. I saw them from an airplane for the first time a year ago to the day. I take the news as I generally take stories of plane crashes. 'Poor bastards. I wonder how many are dead? Lunch in a half-hour.'

A few minutes later, my mother calls me. A second plane has hit. Something big is happening. I stayed tuned to RTÉ radio, awaiting updates. All over Arthur Andersen, people are in a spin, trying to find out more information. Some people were talking to colleagues in the Twin Towers that morning when the phone lines went dead in mid-conversation. Reports of a car-bomb at the US State Department come through. Then reports of another plane crash at the Pentagon in Washington, D.C. An hour later, through a combination of radio, internet, telephone and casual conversations with information seekers/ dispensers, we learn that seven planes have been hi-jacked, the White House is burning, and Camp David is under attack. Most of these 'truths' will later prove unfounded. George W. Bush is apparently flying around America like a coward looking for the deepest hole to hide in. News comes through of another attack on Pittsburgh. Pittsburgh?!

What is in Pittsburgh? I can't figure this one out. There are predictions of 50,000 dead. Wow. I wonder if I know any of them.

A scene from the movie *Pearl Harbour* flashes suddenly through my brain. An American squadron leader tells his pilots in reference to an upcoming mission to Tokyo that if it is his decision, and he knows his plane is not going to make it, he'll pick out a juicy downtown target and ram his craft into it.

I call Marie's mom in Minnesota. It takes about ten attempts for the call to go through. Things are no better there. The grapevine has also erroneously reported an attack on Camp David. My brother sends a text message to my mobile. 'Bet you this is that Bin Laden guy'.

News filters through that one tower has collapsed. Then the other.

It has all been too much to take in. Most of the people in the building have either gone to the pub or home to watch Sky News. I go to the bathroom to splash water over my face. As I look up from the sink, I see my tie, and realise what they have done. Not being able to attack America directly, they – whoever 'they' are – have attacked its symbols.

***

What follows both shocks and inspires the world. America has been attacked by ideologues. In response, ordinary Americans re-discover their own ideologies – democracy, freedom, liberty. It is a reaffirmation of the ideals of the Republic and should have been the beginning of a new Enlightenment. It should have been the beginning of a movement that stood *contra* to the terrorists – an American ideology of Liberty, waging peace and leading by example. It should have returned America to its roots – not a country, but a land in which all are born equal with the right to pursue life, liberty and justice, just as its founders intended.

Instead, George W. reached for his gun.

America does not stop to examine why these attacks occurred. After all, 3000 innocents have been murdered and the government does not allow the people to look for true motive – the first rule of a murder investigation. Instead, the people are told that terrorists have attacked America, because it stands for freedom and they do not. This is a lie. America may once have stood for freedom. Now it appears to represent to many a land of capitalism gone mad, where the dollar reigns supreme. America began as the land of opportunity and ended up as the land of opportunists. It is this America that the terrorists are attacking. America could have looked for some good to come from this dark moment in its history. It could have stopped and shown the terrorists that they were wrong not only in deed, but also in motive, by demonstrating to the world all that America stands for.

But nothing changes. Things move too quickly for the people to think. They are told what they should think and things move on. Instead of the people coming together and showing the world that the terrorists are wrong, America picks a few countries – at random in some cases, it seems, and bombs the shit out of them. Now, instead of the American people saying 'This Is What I Am', American guns are saying 'This Is What We Do'. This is the message heard by the world. The opportunity for soul searching and re-affirmation of core American values disappears, and in its place is a perpetual, vague 'War on Terror' – opportunity for the opportunists.

All of this saddens me. I have a genuine liking for the average American. They face and overcome daily problems with humour and aplomb. They work hard and like to succeed. They know how to enjoy life. But the people at the top are different, doing all they can to squeeze every cent from every niche, the bigger the bank balance the bigger the penis. They do not let many join them at the top. Thus, government elections, for example, can only be won by candidates who are 'one of them', and 'they' rarely have the best interests of the people at heart. But they have enough money and power to spin whatever they want; the masses never truly find out the full story. What I am trying to say, in short, is that the people leading America are a different breed of people to the average American. And this is a shame. Because of this, the ideals and ideas of mainstream America are ignored and new ideas are spun in their place by the powerful. This is why a re-affirmation of the founding American values was not allowed to happen: the people at the top had too much to lose by opening the doors up to true democracy.

***

Let me share a secret with you. On my first day in Arthur Andersen, I am asked to shred a big pile of paper. Not six months later, the company is in trouble – mainly because documents pertaining to some questionable work are...shredded. I want to set the record straight. It is a regional American office that is at fault – not the Irish (or any other offices) – not me.

Andersen is (or was) an American company, founded just after the Great War. Arthur himself opened his offices in the Midwest – in Chicago, Illinois. He established a company renowned for its integrity and incorruptible reputation. By the time I join, there are some 85,000 employees worldwide.

Arthur himself, although long dead, is, by the time I joined, a poster boy for the company. Disney has Mickey Mouse. KFC has the Colonel. We have Arthur. He represents the values which he instilled in his company. His name was synonymous with integrity. He is the face of the brand.

But inside the company, in America, all was not well. Arthur had long since gone. Now, money ruled the day. Promotions began to be based not on integrity, but on income. A cut-throat environment evolved. Soon, it was not uncommon for employees in Andersen's American offices to cut corners and bend the rules in order to make a profit and increase their Christmas bonus.

While all of this was going on, Arthur's good name was being used to cover it up. After all, Arthur was a man of integrity. By association, people thought that the company must be too.

Arthur Andersen, for all intents and purposes, went out of business in 2002. In America, an amazing, yet predictable, thing occurred. Basically, most of the people involved in the illegal accounting practices that led to the fall got off scot-free – despite the fact that the company's activities led to millions being wiped from pension funds all across the USA. A few laws are passed to try to tighten up accountancy procedures. The government seem to be doing something. Therefore the public stop asking questions.

I am most unhappy at the responses of both the American government and the corporate world. We are led to believe that there was a problem, and it was solved. But that is not the case. For companies all over the Western World, profit is the 'be all and end all'. It is the reason they operate. How big a profit can we make in the shortest time possible? Arthur Andersen, the man, showed that there is another way – quality first and the profits will follow.

When the Andersen debacle happened, it sent shock waves through the business community, such was the scale of the issue. The business community should have seized the opportunity to look at how they do business – to re-examine and re-affirm the values of Arthur Andersen himself. A chance to start again.

But this does not happen. Instead, it is treated as if it was an isolated problem. Just as with the great opportunity that should have been taken from the terrorist attacks to measure the current direction of America against its founding ideals, so too is there a missed opportunity – whether intentional or not – to save the corporate soul.

I genuinely have no doubt that when future historians examine these times, they will look on the beginning of the 21st century as the Age of Missed Opportunity. The blame for this can only lie at the door of those who lead. The American people elect them to do something. Instead, they do nothing – but pretend they have not. People will always tend to trust the spinner in the Age of Spin.

CHAPTER SEVEN

Marriage and Insects

In mid-June 2002, a plane carrying Marie and myself leaves London for Chicago. We flew in from Ireland earlier that morning. From London, it will be a nine-hour flight during which we will fly over Greenland, Canada and the Great Lakes. The in-flight movie is *The Perfect Storm* – an odd choice, I think, given that the craft will be flying over the North Atlantic. The flight itself is relatively uneventful. The plane touches down at Chicago O'Hare – one of the world's busiest airports. I have returned to the United States of America.

Marriage is the reason that we have returned – not our own, but the marriage of Marie's best friends and her sister. Not to each other, you understand. After all, this is Minnesota – not Utah.

I will have to clear Immigration in Chicago this time round. London Heathrow does not have a US Immigration desk (as Dublin does). If I am refused entry for any reason, I will have to face a nine-hour return flight.

Marie and I separate – she joins the queue for US citizens, I join a long queue of non-citizens. There are about twenty people ahead of me – but I can't find the five-émigrés-or-less queue. And then a very peculiar thing happens.

From a door at the rear comes a security guard and a beagle – the beagle patrol. In search of narcotics and dog treats, no doubt. The friendly looking little dog is being handled by a not-so-friendly looking woman – mid-thirties, no smile. The dog walks in between people, touching his snout to bags and luggage items.

The little dog briefly sniffs my bag. He continues on. Lucky that I have left my stash of heroin-laced Eukanuba [dog food] at home [This is a 'joke']. There is a youngish guy standing in front of me in the queue. He looks to be a French backpacker-type person – although I'm quite sure that he is neither. The little dog sniffs him, and sits beside him. A treat comes from the handler's pocket for the little dog.

"Sir. Can you please remove your back pack?" asks the handler as she pulls it from his back.

"Sir. Can you please open your back pack?" asks the handler as she unzips it.

"Sir. Can you please take out the contents of the back pack?" asks the handler as she removes the contents.

I am, by now intrigued. Actually – I am more than intrigued. I am worried. Is it a bomb? Will he put up a fight? Will he take someone hostage to protect his narcotics stash? If he grabs a hostage, it will either be me or the dog handler – and no one is going to care if Mrs No-Smiles is grabbed. Oh shit. I am potentially in trouble.

The French backpacker isn't saying a word. He is acting very, very calm. Shit. Then, the handler finds what she is looking for. Slowly, she removes a plastic bag with a mysterious object rumpled inside of it. She looks at the French guy.

"Sir. Could you please remove this from the bag?"

Well – here goes. Am I about to see a drugs bust – which would be kinda cool – or become a hostage – involuntarily, I might add – which would not be so cool. Actually, there is a third option that I have not yet considered. What if there is nothing illegal in the bag – or something that is only technically illegal, like meat or vegetables or something? Will he be willing to take a hostage to protect his pork chops or his rack of lamb?

Option three turns out to be the closest. What he has in his bag is technically a meat product – although one that it is not technically illegal to bring into the USA. He opens the plastic bag…and pulls out a pile of un-rolled, used, pink bandages – many with blood clots. It is repulsive. And there are so many. Did the plane crash while I was asleep?

I suspect that the possession of old smelly bandages at an Immigration point is not illegal. I am right. He is let go, and the beagle lady moves on, no doubt intending not to smile a little more that day.

Soon, I am at the head of the queue.

"Where are you going?" asks the gruff looking Immigration official.

"Minnesota."

"Minnesota? What's in Minnesota?"

"My girlfriend's sister is getting married."

"And what – are you here to stop the wedding or something?"

"That depends – I've not met the sister yet."

It works. He laughs.

"Hey Gerry – get over here."

Over waddles his Immigration official friend.

"Is there a problem here?"

"No – he's here for a wedding. I asked him if he is here to stop it. He said he don't know – he hasn't met the bride yet."

"Ha ha ha – you Irish crack me up."

OK. Very funny…but I am in.

I meet up with Marie on the other side. We need to go to another Terminal. We move quickly, lest one of the massively obese people that populate the airport think that we are not fit and in our prime and pick us off for lunch.

We make it to the inter-Terminal shuttle train service. A massively, massively obese man in an airport worker's uniform – no older than ourselves (the man, not the uniform) – is orchestrating matters at the stop. I am bemused by the fact that this is his job. Most people are having a hard time manoeuvring their luggage around him.

Within two hours, we are on our way again – Chicago to Minneapolis. Eight hours by car or train – but only one and a half by plane. Chicago is hot – 100°F. Minneapolis is even hotter. As we step from the plane onto the jetway at Minneapolis-St Paul International, we bake. It is *sooooo* hot.

Marie's sister meets us at the Terminal – not the one that we are there to see married, but Gertie, now an expert, thanks to me and my first bout of jet lag two years earlier, in dendrochronological phrenology. We walk into the car park. It is getting hotter by the step. The car park – although roofed – is open air. The heat kicks the soul out of me and will, for the next two weeks, take its place. Why is it so hot? It was -40°C the last time I was here. Now it is almost forty above?! I soon come to the conclusion that they have forgotten to take in the snow after winter. Now, it is rotting, and giving off heat.

***

There is something else. Something I had not really seen before, but had merely glimpsed. Two years ago, when I first arrived and was unpacking, I felt something on my arm. Looking down, I saw a mosquito. I had never seen a real mosquito before. I watched in fascination as it did what mosquitoes do. It was amazing to me – this is the little creature that I had heard so much about on TV programmes and in books from other countries. I looked closely at its make up as it drank from my skin. What an interesting little creature it is. I pondered the mysteries and beauty of Nature as I squashed him into a pulped mess.

Winter had come soon after. Thus, that mosquito was practically all that I had seen of American wildlife. I visited the Bell Museum of Natural History in the Twin Cities – but it just wasn't the same.

Our plan for this vacation is to spend a few days in the Cities before heading North to Duluth. Recently, while driving through the Phoenix Park in Dublin, a squirrel scampered across the road in front of the car.

"Marie – look! Look! A squirrel! Do you see it? Do you see it?"

"Oh yeah – it's only a squirrel, though," said Marie as I panted to catch my breath.

"What do you mean?"

"Wait until we go to the Twin Cities this summer. Then you'll see squirrels."

"But we have lots of squirrels in Ireland."

"No, you don't."

Yet again, as she usually is, Marie was right. In Ireland, squirrels are a furry friend that we see occasionally. They brighten up the rare day upon which we see them. In the Twin Cities however, things are different. There is no such thing as an occasional squirrel – unless it is in a wedding dress or lighting fireworks on the Fourth of July. The Cities are – literally – infested with them. The squirrels are mangy. They are flea-ridden. They are in their tens of thousands. They are in the trees. They are on the lawns. They are on balconies and on the roads. In Ireland, as kids, we sat around and devised plans to capture a squirrel – a furry chum that we could cuddle and take to school in our pockets. We never did capture one. In America – where there is ample opportunity to catch as many as would be needed to fill pockets of any volume, the desire to do so is underwhelming. For starters, their tails are not big and bushy. They are sparse and wiry. They do not forage around beneath trees and bushes for nuts and berries. Instead they rummage through bins and barbecues looking for scraps of cheeseburgers and potato chips. Cuddling them is not an option unless prescribed by Jack Kevorkian [Dr Death, euthanasia advocate] himself. If this is what urban America is like, what will the rural area to the north of Duluth be like? I will find out in just a few short days – and will wish for the squirrels again.

All I know about American wildlife I learned from TV. I know that bears eat stupid children whose parents send them over to feed the bear ice cream while they stand by with their video cameras. I know that moose roam around the northern half of the country, living off grass and the contents of trashcans. I have heard about raccoons – something else we do not have back home – although Americans do get a kick out of the fact that Dublin Zoo has a raccoon enclosure. But that is pretty much all I know. I would soon experience the best and the worst of American wildlife.

The best – or one of the best – comes just two days later. We bid farewell to the Twin Cities and head north – a friend is driving us to Duluth, and to Marie's mom's house. As the car turns around the last corner onto the final mile of road before the house, we see something.

Not 50 metres in front of the car, padding across the road with an almost leisurely manner, is a wild American Bobcat. It is magnificent, about the size of a small German Shepherd dog: a cat that big, living in the wilds of Minnesota. I am awe-struck – the image has lived with me ever since.

We slow the car down and open up the windows. Soon, he disappears into the surrounding forest. But we almost immediately encounter the worst of American wildlife. As the awe subsides, we heard something. *Pop. Pop.* What the hell is that popping sound? It seems to be coming from the tyres of the car – from the road. We only notice it because we have reduced our speed to a crawl and have the windows open. It sounds as if the road surface is bubbling – as if we are driving across melting bubble wrap.

"Do you hear that popping noise?" asks the friend who is driving.

"That's the sound of the car tyres crushing the Army Worms."

Now, Army Worms are forest tent caterpillars. In Northern Minnesota, they are on a seven-year cycle meaning that for six years they are not seen. But the seventh year…there is a good reason that local Minnesotans know them as 'Army Worms'. To say that you have seen a lot of caterpillars does not really capture it. To say that you have seen a plague of Army Worms is a bit closer to the truth. An army of insects has overtaken the northern half of the State. I have never seen a plague before – only read about them in the Bible. But here is the mother of them all. The great Army Worm plague of '02.

It is very, very difficult to do justice to describing the scale of the plague. Scientists estimate that the Army Worms are in their *trillions*. The locals have to resort to using *snow shovels* to clear their drives and decks of them. It is impossible to walk *at all* without stepping on five or six with each foot. The State even distributes instructions on careful driving – the chances of skidding on the greasy bodies of a dead platoon of Army Worms and crashing is so great! They are *everywhere*. They crawl over house walls – although, interestingly enough, drive through suburbia and it is possible to tell which houses are using lead free paint. Another term for 'Lead Free' is 'Army Worm Friendly' – a term that marketing departments rarely use in ad campaigns.

Entire forests lie bare, stripped of all foliage in mid-June. Entire eco-systems are displaced – no leaves to eat. The bird population is, however, thriving, as is the population of small mammals.

The locals tell me that although this happens every seven years, they can't recall it being so bad. Hardly surprising, I think, since the introduction of GM crops in the fields that are their traditional breeding grounds has left the moths to find new places to lay their eggs.

Now, it is bad enough having to remove your shoes before going into the house so as not to smush dead Army Worms into the carpet. It is bad enough having to wear socks despite the sweltering heat of over 35°C. It is bad enough that cooking on the barbecue means Nature will invariably add some extra protein and greasy flavour. But worst of all is the fact that the Army Worms spin threads.

The Army Worms – when not devastating forests or causing car crashes – literally just hang around. They crawl into tall trees, attach a line, and spin down to about human shoulder height – hanging there. Every walk under a tree becomes a gauntlet run. Army Worms on threads stick to my hair. They attach to my T-shirt. They fall down my neck.

It happens no matter how careful I am. When it comes to thread spinning, spiders (no matter what one thinks of them) are masters. They build amazingly strong, symmetrical, anchored designs that they can manipulate to best effect. Have you ever seen a spider lose his/her footing?

Army Worms, however, are different. They only spin one strand from which to dangle. Thus, should anything untoward happen during hanging time they, lacking vigilance, simply and lazily fall – usually onto me.

This means that despite the sweltering heat, a walk in the local park is out of the question. It means that children, unless dressed in 1930s diving costumes, cannot climb trees. It means that risking skin cancer from overexposure to the sun is preferable to seeking the shade of a tall, infested tree. A barefoot walk on the cool grass is a non-starter. Since the

Army Worms are as green as the grass itself, it is impossible to tell what – or whom – would be stepped upon.

Undressing at night has become a trial. There is always an Army Worm crawling around my penis trunk looking for leaves or pulsating across my stomach looking for a place to attach and hang from. Nor is it a simple matter of flicking them away. They have sticky feet. They must to be picked up between thumb and forefinger and pulled – each leg releasing its sticky grip in turn – until all are free. It will then curl into a ball or pulsate in the peristaltic manner in which they walk. It is a delicate balancing act. Too much finger pressure means that they *pop* – and, in a variation on the ad, once you pop it, you can't stop it. The greasy contents – organs etc. – poo onto fingers. Soap and hot water time.

In the end, there are so many that there is simply not enough food to sustain the massive population. They die in their millions. For a brief period, the roads stink as the greasy surface rots in the hot, hot sun. A few seem to turn cannibal – but hopefully this is merely for survival and not just for kicks. A couple of weeks after our trip, word comes that the plague has subsided. I hope that I've done justice to it – that I've given a good impression of what it was like. I like to add that I still wake up at night screaming as I dream of them falling from trees down my shirt, or getting tangled in the webs of several at once. It seems to me that it would do it justice. But rather than victim, I will play the part of survivor – the one who lived to tell the tale of the great plague of summer '02.

***

We have two weddings to attend – one on each Saturday of our trip. Seems like good opportunity to tie the knot ourselves. So we do.

We go to the Duluth courthouse, where we each hold our right hands in the air and swear that we are who we claim to be and that we are not married to anyone else. We are issued with a licence. Simple as that.

We arrange to meet a judge at a spot on Brighton Beach on the shores of Lake Superior at 11.00 a.m. on the morning of 19 June. But all is not to go exactly to plan. We don't have much – or any – time to organise a wedding: a few hours to be precise. This is in stark contrast with Marie's sister who is to be married the following Saturday in a proper ceremony. Whether it was right or not, we decide not to let the sister know until after her own wedding. We don't want her to think that we are taking anything away from her big day – after all, hers has been months in the planning.

We tell the judge that if there are any problems, he is not – under any circumstances – to call the home phone. Marie's yet-to-be-married sister is staying here this week and we don't want her to know. Under no circumstances is he to call the house.

At 10.00 a.m., he calls the house. Marie's to-be-married sister answers the phone and promptly tells him that something is wrong. She is indeed getting married in Duluth – but not until Saturday.

We have no choice but to come clean. We tell her that we are to be married within the hour. She is genuinely thrilled – I guess that we should have just told her from the beginning.

We manage to put the word out and assemble a crowd of eight to meet us at the Victorian bandstand on the beach. It is a beautiful spot – rugged, rocky and overlooking the serenely beautiful waters of Superior. The weather has been beautiful all summer – not a cloud in the sky. It is going to be picture perfect.

At ten minutes to eleven – still not sure if the judge has received the 'Wedding-is-back-on' memo that we left with his wife – we arrive at the bandstand on Brighton Beach. It is raining. A thick fog has descended over the shoreline. The sunshine of the morning, however, will be provided by Marie's younger sister, who has managed, at the last minute, to rent an Elvis costume – that wonderful Las Vegas touch. I am getting married in America.

The ceremony itself is very pleasant. The judge – a retired, elderly man whose grandmother was a Malone from Dublin – gives a nice speech filled with advice garnered from his own experience of marriage, of how it is a partnership, and that shouldn't be forgotten. It is a good solid message upon which to begin a marriage, I think.

Not having wedding rings, we use two of Marie's finger rings – a Claddagh and a pinkie ring studded with holes. I place – sorry – ram the ring onto Marie's ring finger. Then it is my turn. I hand her my right hand – but the judge says nothing. The Claddagh barely clears my fingernail. I pretend that it is on all the way, and the ceremony concludes.

Our friends and family take pictures of us standing on the beach, huddled together beneath a Dunne's Stores black umbrella. I think that the pictures hold a certain charm. We then thank the judge, and walk to a nearby picnic area, where we eat the Subway subs that Marie's mom has picked up on the way.

As a surprise, Marie's mom has booked us a night in a cabin about an hour up the North Shore of the lake. The cabin is in between the rather ominously named towns of Castle Danger and Knife River. Is this a sign?

The cabin turns out to be absolutely delightful. It is on a relatively untouched part of the North Shore – quite close to the amazingly good New Scenic Café. The cabin has been built on the lake – the waters of Superior lap up beneath the floor. The cabin is as rustic as they come – a small kitchen and a large bedroom. No TV or need for electrical appliances, for example. Its best feature is the window. The entire wall looking out onto the lake is a window! The bed faces out onto the lake itself. After a walk along the rocky shoreline, we retire for the night. I relish being able to look out on the shore all night – watching ships pass by and the flickering of distant porch lights on the far side. This mental image is, however, not what I see. Instead, we are treated to the most amazing electrical storm I have ever witnessed. All night, we look out from our bed onto the lake as it flashes purple like electricity and orange like fire. It is awe-inspiring. America has not let me down.

The next morning we wake to our first day as man and wife, woman and husband. The only food in the cabin is…corn, which we peel, cook, and eat.

***

A funny thing happens just before the first of the weddings that week. Marie's best friends are getting married – another outdoor wedding. It will take place in the beautiful rose garden at Leif Erickson Park overlooking Duluth. Marie is to be bridesmaid – meaning that I will not see her until later that afternoon.

The weather is spectacular – everyone there develops a tan by noon and skin cancer by evening. Rather than hang around for an hour and wait in the heat for the wedding to begin, Marie's younger sister and I decide to go for a stroll. We go to DeWitt-Seitz – an upmarket, touristy shopping area at the far end of the park. We enter a shop that sells crap – Native American Dream Catchers, Duluth Thimbles, local recipe books. You know the kind. Gertie and I pause to look at bottles of local maple syrup. Nearby, we see two tourists – women, mid-forties – looking at a clothing rack. The rack is filled with lace knit sweaters – the kind that cannot be worn on their own as they look like a moth with a sense of symmetry has had a go at them.

One woman pulls on such a sweater over her tank top.

"Well – what do you think?"

"Oh – don't buy this one – I can see a loose thread hanging from it."

"Oh – don't pull at it. It's not a thread. That's just my skin. It's been peeling badly for a couple of days now."

And with that, she removes the garment, hangs it back on the rack, and moves on to another section of the shop. Nice!

The wedding itself goes off perfectly. It seems that American weddings are not all that different to Irish weddings – a ceremony followed by a good ol' knees-up. There are, in fact, only a couple of things that are different or new.

Not long into the wedding reception, I hear a spoon being tapped against a glass. This is repeated until around half the guests are doing the same.

'Speech time,' I guess. I guess wrong. The bride and groom – each talking to different groups of guests – run over to each other and kiss.

Hmm.

About five minutes later, it happens again. Glasses tapped, no speech, kissing. *Hmm.* I inquire about it. Turns out that it is an American wedding tradition – wait until the most inopportune moment to make the bride and groom have to seek each other out to kiss. And they seem to be enjoying the little tradition, as are the crowd.

It happens again. And again. Wow – this looks like fun. Maybe this is a good time to continue my direct participation with American culture. My first attempt at direct involvement was more of a public service duty – warning the locals against the dangers of jaywalking in downtown St Paul. It did not go down too well. Thus, I will seek redemption through participation in this tradition – it must surely help my quest for acceptance.

I have a glass of white wine in front of me. I take a spoon, and hold it between the tips of my thumb and index finger. I hold it aloft. And I wait. The bride and groom are too close together. Not yet. Not yet.

Soon, the opportunity presents itself. The couple stand about 40 feet from each other, talking to different people. Here goes – my latest direct contribution to American society. *Clink. Clink.*

My lonely clinks go unaccompanied. *Clink. Clink.* A couple of people without clinking implements turn to look at me. Shit. Now I have to continue – I can't abort. *Clink. Clink.* Nothing. What the hell am I doing wrong? This is embarrassing. By now, about a dozen or so people have noticed my hermetic clinks. They are, however, not joining in. To my relief, Marie notices me from the head table (bridesmaid's perk), and joins in. Soon, the room is clinking – albeit without the same panache that had been shown to the American entrepreneurs of clink during the past hour. What the hell have I done wrong?

The bride and groom begin searching for each other. Well, at least *they* enjoyed my cultural contribution, right? The groom is not smiling. The bride somehow knows that this round is my fault. She shoots a mean glare in my direction that scares the Dickens out of my clinking finger. What is going on? They kiss – but this time it is a chore.

To this day, I'm not sure what I did wrong. But whatever it was, the room knew it. Perhaps I chose the wrong rhythm. Perhaps I chose the wrong key in which to start. Perhaps I simply shouldn't have done it and stuck to things that I actually know about such as the do's and don'ts of jaywalking.

The meal is served, and the band – the Sensational Joint Chiefs – a really excellent Minneapolis band – strike up with 'The Girl From Ipanema'. I kind of know how the girl must have felt – the song is a song about things the girl does – walking, etc. I'm sure that my clinking activities are equally as noteworthy.

The older crowd retires, leaving a small but dedicated crowd of twenty-somethings behind – with approximately two bottles of champagne each to consume. It is a nice evening of live Jazzy Funk and soft bubbling sweetness. I try to dance with Marie – but thanks to the fact that I have inherited my father's dancing genes and not those of a better dancer (Stephen Hawking, for example), Marie soon gives up – despite the fact I even remove my shoes and socks so as not to stomp on her. Again. Some of the couples on the dance floor mysteriously disappear to the bathroom together. I wonder why. The rest each have a bottle of champagne in their hands, a song in their mouths and a dance floor under their feet. Twenty-somethings don't change – no matter where they come from. They are interested in alcohol, music and sex – even though I have serious misgivings about some of them. I'm thinking in particular of a funk-dancer who could only have been taught to dance by my father who seems to have too much knowledge of the first, no appreciation of the second and no experience of the third.

We wait until the wee hours of the morning before going home. I did not experience anything American today – merely something human.

***

The following weekend, we attend the wedding of Marie's older sister. With the three weddings, there is not much else we can squeeze in to the trip. We try to venture out a couple of times for walks or sightseeing, but it proves too messy with the Army Worm problem.

This is also the summer of the World Cup in Japan and Korea. I am following it avidly – along with about 90 per cent of the world's population. Ireland is doing particularly well. We qualify for the second round before Marie and I depart for America. The next Ireland match will take place during our trip.

'No problem,' I think. 'There's bound to be a satellite channel or a local sports bar that is showing it.' In fact, the USA is doing particularly well – they have beaten Portugal, for example. Great. I wonder how everyone is reacting?

When I reach Duluth, I see no sports flags. I see no soccer jerseys. I see sports bars, but none mention anything about the World Cup. I ask local people – sports fans – about the World Cup. 'Which sport?' The TV listings list *nothing* about it.

I begin to get desperate. It rapidly becomes clear that I will not be able to find a kindred spirit with which to share the agony and ecstasy of watching a World Cup knock-out match. It is also becoming clear that I will be lucky to get to watch the match *at all*. I mobilise friends – people are calling people on my behalf attempting to locate *anyone* who has the match. I have a full week in which to make my preparations.

Nothing.

On the morning of the match, I wake early – I was unable to sleep as I have pre-match jitters. I wait until the last minute – but now it is clear. I will not be able to watch the world's largest sporting event – America just doesn't care.

I do what I have to do, and call my mother. I call her every five minutes to get match updates. She is watching it with the entire family in my grandmother's house. I can hear it: Ireland versus Spain. I can hear the roars of the crowd in the Far East coming down the mouthpiece of an Irish phone to a receiver in the USA. I can feel the emotion of my family through the phone. I can hear their screams. But I cannot see them. All I can see are feckin' Army Worms.

Ireland end up being knocked out thanks to a penalty shoot-out. The country is devastated, and I am deprived of the chance to wallow in the national self-pity.

I have never had much time for American sports – I just never got them, I guess. I've tried to watch American Football, but it looks too much like rugby for the brittle-boned to me. I've tried to watch baseball – which, like cricket, makes me feel like I've taken too many antihistamines. I was even in America during the 2000 Olympics and took verbal slaggings because Ireland ended up with only one medal – although I'm not sure why. One medal for a country of four million people is pretty good going.

The sports scene in America perplexes me. It is strong. It is vibrant. But it is all local. The rest of the international community engages with each other through sports – for example, when Ireland played football in Iran in 2001, the journalists and travellers told us about the people there, about their customs and beliefs. And we understood them a little more and maybe even empathised with them a little. Thus, to a degree, public engagement with international football can prove an educative experience of sorts. The Irish, for example, learned that the Iranian government is not necessarily representative of the opinions of the Iranian people.

In America, the disengagement of the people with international sport – 'soccer' in this case, has robbed them of full participation in international affairs. And here's where I get controversial.

In all of my time in America, there is only one thing that I see that provokes the same national feeling that I have witnessed in other countries in relation to international soccer.

The team is the US Army. The event is a war.

War in America is – as far as I can see – the national sport, or rather the national-international sport. It seems to be the only time when a significant enough section of the population mobilises to follow something international. Thus, it is practically the only time that the media bother to follow international affairs.

This has, it seems, misled many Americans into thinking that America is somehow the pinnacle of world developmental aspiration. It has given them a bit of a superiority complex – every time they go to war, they win – no matter what the actual result. George W. spent a year trying to make a tired, clapped-out Iraqi army and dictator seem like 'the team to beat'. America won the first leg of the match, and the popularity of the manager reached an all-time high.

The rest of the world – or, at least, the people, not the governments or those with the fattest wallets – now psychologically wage war on the soccer field. If they're beaten, it sucks – but there will always be the opportunity to turn the tables next year. It's not too far-fetched to believe that Ireland's defeat of England in the 1988 European Soccer Championships made up for 700 years of English oppression in the minds of many.

In America, it seems impossible to satisfy the public psyche's desire for revenge and Freudian penis measuring contests without the spectacle of a war.

This is, I think, one of the hardest things for me to deal with in America. Criticising war seems as pointless in America as criticising soccer itself rather than the team or the manager, as in the rest of the world. It is a sport – or is, at least, treated as one by those in power and by the public psyche.

By the time I return to the United States in 2002 (my first trip since September 11), America has decided to engage itself in a perpetual War against Terror. There are US flags flying in front of every home. There are billboards depicting the heroes of the 'sport' – firemen, etc. People are signing up to the 'sport' – military volunteering has peaked.

As I write this, that enthusiasm is severely waning. The reason is that the current team manager, Mr Bush, seems to have 'misunderestimated' things. How much enthusiasm would people in Ireland have if the Football Association announced that it was going to play a perpetual football match? People would watch for the first while, but quickly become bored with it. That is what is happening in America, in my opinion. People are used to a quick game, where they win in a discernable time frame. Perpetuity is not such a suitable time frame.

I admit that my conclusion on the American attitude to 'War' will offend some – particularly as I've met and known many, many Americans who are vehemently opposed to war – but the system does not help them to get their viewpoint across.

In Ireland, I estimate that about 66 per cent of the population got behind Ireland during the World Cup. That leaves 33 per cent who have no interest or felt that it is a waste of time. I reckon that the same figures could probably be applied to the 'war' and 'peace' lobbies in the USA.

***

Although the 2002 trip is a mere two-week stay, I feel that I have learned more about the culture than on my 2000 trip. The reason for this is the fact that I have a purpose – a reason for being there. I am a tourist on vacation. In 2000, I was…well, I'm not really sure myself. Now, as a tourist, I feel that I can engage with the people. People can pigeonhole me and will talk freely with me now. They know why I am here this time. They offer me advice on what to do and see. And they ask my opinion on things. As far as I can see it, when someone from the American culture lets a non-American in, you're pretty much in for life. It's a nice American feature – the price of which is allowing yourself to be labelled and quantified.

CHAPTER EIGHT

An American Christmas

I do not return to the USA for another eighteen months. It is an unusual eighteen months during which I am perpetually ill. I have many differing medical tests to try to determine the problem. The tests continue for about nine months, and leave me exhausted. I am in bad need of a vacation. With this in mind, Marie and I decide to return to America to spend Christmas and New Year with her friends and family. I will get the test results shortly after my return.

The trip will again pass through Chicago – although this time we will have the additional hassle of trying to negotiate our way through London's Heathrow en route from Dublin. Personally, I hate large airports. Something always happens to me in them. They are just too big to negotiate around. 'Seán versus the Large Airports' has been a long running saga, ever since I studied for a time in Germany in the last year of the 20th century. My Airport nemeses include Heathrow, Paris Charles de Gaulle, Chicago and the airport that started it all, Frankfurt. Despite using Frankfurt on many, many occasions, I've never had a smooth run – but 1999 was to prove a weird year in the saga. A poor student, I could only afford to travel to Frankfurt on the weekend – despite the fact that the flight would not leave until Monday evening. This meant staying in Frankfurt overnight – and by Frankfurt, I mean the Airport.

It would not be my first time sleeping in an Airport – I spent a very quiet night in Belfast Airport in 1997 with two friends – we were *literally* the only people of any description in the airport all night.

When I get to Frankfurt, I am relieved to see that I am not the only person who has decided to stay the night. In fact, the lobby and corridors are literally thronged with sleeping travellers. It is amazingly quiet – everyone is actually asleep!

At about 2.00 a.m., I wake with the hunger. I need food, but have already eaten my supplies. I leave my bags with a friend, and go off in search of an eatery. I follow the airport signs. Straight ahead. Left. Straight. Right. Left. Straight. Back where I started. Shit. How did that happen? I see a cleaner and ask him if there is anywhere to eat. He nods, and gives me some loose directions. I go straight ahead, up two flights of stairs, turn left and pass through a short corridor. Where am I? In the baggage reclaim area. I have somehow managed to make my way into the wrong side of the Immigration partition. And my passport is back in my bags. After a lot of arguing and haggling in German, the Immigration official decides to re-admit me. I decide to give up and go back to my bags. As I tiptoe quietly through the sleeping corridors – slumbering dreamers scattered all around me on the floors – I spot an ice-cream vending machine. I ask my stomach if ice cream will be acceptable. It says 'yes'. The vending machine is essentially a giant clown-shaped device that oozes ice cream from a hole in its stomach into a cone.

Silently, I place the money into the coin slot – cringing as it crashes noisily into the moneybox within. A few people stir slightly. A button lights up. I am to press it when I want my cone – which I duly do.

Suddenly the clown lights up. Hidden speakers blare into life, singing, "I scream – you scream – we all scream for ice-cream." All around me, angry Germans are waking up and shooting death-wish glares in my direction. And still the clown continues. "I scream – you scream…" The ice-cream oozing part now buzzes loudly into action. Babies and children now start to wake, looking at the weird spectacle of an Irishman feeding from a clown at 2.30 a.m. I grab the finished cone and run away. The clown does not stop singing for another ten or so minutes.

The next day, my resentment towards this airport grows as the airline charge me IR£150 for excess baggage – despite the fact that this is the fourth time I have transported this same baggage with the airline this year and not encountered a charge before.

On my way to Minnesota at Christmas 2003, Heathrow continues the offensive against me. Off the first flight, we attempt to find our way to the second. Soon, in from the jetway, we begin to see signs for the Flight Connections Centre. Left. Then right. Walking. Walking. Walking for an awfully long time. More signs for the Flight Connections Centre. Must be on the right track, so.

We turn a corner and see a door. A sign beside it tells us that we are now leaving the 'backstage' area, and would need to clear Customs. Hmm…I stop an airport worker to ask him where we are supposed to go. He points down a nearby corridor, telling us to take the elevator down a floor.

Relieved, we duly do this and, sure enough, we soon see more signs for the Flight Connections Centre. Great. After about another ten minutes of walking and following signs, we end up back at the point where the airport worker had given us directions.

We now see another sign for the Flight Connections Centre, one that we have not seen before. It hangs in an area that leaves us even more confused than before. Beneath it, there is a corridor, a stairwell and a door. What are we to do?

We take a chance, and use the door. Wrong option. We are now in the Flight Check-in area. We have entered the UK without having seen any Immigration officials. This could pose a problem.

We approach the desk of the airline we are due to continue our flight with. They tell us that this is the incorrect Check-in desk for our particular flight and that it seems that we are already checked in and should proceed to the Flight Connections Centre. Hmm. We tell them of our dilemma. They point to a small, unnoticed corridor in the corner.

We go in. There is only one sign here: Flight Connections Centre. Hooray! The area that we are in is not the Centre itself – merely a lobby-type area. A woman working behind the counter looks at our tickets and motions for us to go down an adjacent corridor, down a flight of stairs and through a door.

Not five minutes later, we are back in the Check-in area – having somehow evaded Immigration for a second time that day.

An airport security worker sees us and approaches us. He asks what we are looking for, then delivers us – personally – to where we are supposed to be. He checks our passports – why is there no stamp on Marie's from UK Immigration? This is going to be a long day.

Soon, however, we are on our way again. We take our seats in the Boeing 777 – a magnificent aircraft in which we have not flown before. We have seen in-flight movies before, but have never had our own individual screens, such as this craft offers. London to Chicago looks promising.

Soon after this behemoth of a craft takes off – or rather, lifts off – a stewardess hands out headphones with which we can listen to our tiny screens. We will have a choice of ten movies. Great! Marie chooses *Monsters Inc.* – a movie that we have not yet seen. What will I watch? I take my remote control and press the menu button. Nothing happens. I press it again. Still, nothing happens. Maybe it's touch-screen activated. I press a greasy thumb against the screen. Nope. Not touch-activated. Hmm – maybe the entertainment system has not kicked in yet. I ask Marie if hers has started yet.

"Marie. Marie?" I shout/whisper.

She does not hear me.

"Marie. Marie!"

She can't hear me, as she is engrossed in her movie. I'll ask her later when she isn't busy.

I grab a passing stewardess. Poor word choice – I ask a passing stewardess if she knows what is wrong with my entertainment system. She does. *Great!* It is broken. Great – at least I know what is wrong. She looks at my screen.

"Did you press your thumb against the screen?"

Hundreds of seats and I get the broken one. No matter, though. At least I have a good book to read. Shit. I packed it. That means one thing – a nine-hour flight armed with only an in-flight magazine and the newspaper I purchased the day before – the *Weekly World News*.

Because of this, although Marie and I arrive into Chicago on the same flight, my journey seems to take about twenty times longer. No matter, though. I am in Chicago – and in the USA – with an entire two hours to kill before our next flight.

Not that we don't have things to do – in America, all bags have to be brought through Customs at the first airport of entry. This means collecting and re-checking our luggage. We walk through Customs. No problems. However, when we get to the area where we are to re-check our bags, there is a queue. Now, I'm not a very good judge of queues, but I say that there are about a million people here. An Air India flight to Mumbai is leaving that evening. All of the people who will be on it are now in the queue ahead of me. Great.

An American airport security official approaches us after about five minutes of waiting.

"You two – this way."

Shit. What have we done now?

"I'll check your bags for you. Can't have you waiting in line behind all of these wogs."

'What did he say? Did he actually say what I *think* he said?' I am in a quandary now. If I say anything, I will have airport security on my ass. I'll probably not be allowed to fly and could even be arrested for challenging them under that damn USA PATRIOT Act (Uniting and Strengthening America by Providing Appropriate Tools Required to Intercept and Obstruct Terrorism). On the other hand, I can't let him get away with blatant racism, can I – racism that has been instigated to *serve me*? What kind of person would I be if I let this happen?

Realising that having married into an American family means frequent trips to the USA, and that I have to keep Immigration on my good side, I choose the first option, and keep my damn mouth shut. I have allowed practical concerns to govern my principles and it is very disconcerting. Our bags are rechecked, and we are sent on our way with a smile and a 'Have a nice day'. Although the rest of the people in line have paid the same airport fees as I have, they are not afforded the same privileges. Sick to my stomach about what I have – or have not – done, I move on and find my gate.

A couple of hours later, we arrive in Minneapolis-St Paul International Airport. Marie's sisters and friends are there to greet us. This is the America I have come to see. As we leave the airport car park, a temperature sign reads -24°F. It is snowing. Driving through central Minneapolis, the car soon comes to a halt to allow a Christmas parade to pass. Christmas in America – my first. We drive to the apartment of Marie's older sister, where we will be staying for a couple of days before heading up to Duluth.

***

Christmas in Middle America. December. Snow. Ice. I find it...different. In Ireland, Christmas is everywhere. It has been in my face since late September through to mid-January. There is no respite from it. In America, the Christmas season is decidedly shorter. It does not begin until Thanksgiving – late November – and lasts only until Christmas itself.

I find Christmas in America to be far less artificial than it is at home. It is about doing things, more so than getting things. Take visiting Santa. For the same price as visiting Santa in a shopping mall in Ireland, it is possible to take the Duluth Scenic Railroad – or the Polar Express as it has been seasonally re-labelled – along a five-mile stretch of frozen Lake Superior to see Santa at his grotto. It is the experience that counts – unlike the measly present that Santa doles out to kids in malls back home.

I think that most kids, if given the choice, would prefer the event. I can vividly remember the last time that I saw Santa as a kid. It was in a hotel close to our house. The extended family had decided to try eating away from home that Christmas Day. About halfway through the dry meal, in walked a Dubliner – on the wrong side of fifty and on the wrong side of bronchitis – dressed as a very shabby Santa. His suit had been cobbled together. A very long time ago. His beard, thin, fake, yellowing.

In Ireland, we always left out a bottle of stout for Santa. Until then, I hadn't realised that he'd also have liked twenty Marlboro and a Ventolin inhaler. Santa approached our table. He reached into his stained sack – which, as I gauged from the gifts received by other children in the room, is filled with a multitude of crap – and produced a deck of cards.

"Here you go, son," he growled in his hungover, gruff Dublin accent. "Be a gambler."

Although I do not go on the Polar Express that year, I do not imagine that the American Santa Claus would be quite like this.

***

At first, looking back on Christmas in America, I think it unusual that there seems to be a lack of materialism – that people want to do things together, rather than to give things to each other. There seems to be something wrong with this dichotomy. After all – aren't Americans the driving force behind world materialist consumerism? And isn't Christmas the ultimate tribute to this?

I had seen the same at Hallowe'en – there were parties etc. that had been set up for children. The biggest that I saw took place at Camp Snoopy in the Mall of America, where I imagined thousands of little witches, wizards, Power Rangers and Nixons would gather to celebrate the occasion.

However, when Hallowe'en came around, there were no witches. There were fewer wizards. Nixon was absent. There were, however, Power Rangers. There were Spider-Men. There was even the occasional Scooby-Doo. Frankenstein was there, but he was smiling. So too was Dracula.

What was going on? I had vaguely noticed this about Hallowe'en a few years earlier, but had not been able to put my finger on it. I just had a feeling – I wasn't even sure about what. Now, at Christmas time, the feeling returns. What, though, have the Power Rangers got to do with the Polar Express?

And then it hits me. Mainstreaming. Control. Fear. Dracula is too scary for our kids. Let's make him smile. Better yet, let's make the kids dress up as TV stars – get rid of the nasty side of Hallowe'en, but keep the pleasure of dressing up.

But let's go further than that. Let's outsource the venue – outsource the experience. I cannot let anything go wrong with my child's Christmas or Hallowe'en, or else they'll be screwed up and have to see a shrink when they are older. I'll pay for the perfect experience. I'll pay to have Hallowe'en in Camp Snoopy and Christmas on the Polar Express. I'll buy memories – the memories that I want my child to have.

On the face of it, there's nothing really wrong with parents wanting the best for their children. In fact, I don't want to meet the parent that doesn't. Where I see a problem is in the supply of on-demand memories – a purchasable emotion for every occasion. Will this generation of Americans grow up not knowing how to create memories of their own? What problems will come when people realise that life is not managed for them – that not everything turns out like the Polar Express? My drunken smoker Santa played a small part in helping me to realise that although things are not always what they are supposed to be, it is not necessarily a bad thing. I got a smile and a story out of him. I wonder how this unscripted, post-modernist Santa would have gone down in the US, where the Christmas destination seems to always be 34th Street?

This type of memory management is creeping into Ireland and the rest of the world as I write. Its effect on society will be measured by how people react when the script breaks down. Will they get a smile out of Santa telling the kid to be a gambler, or protest to the manager if something happens that is not in the script?

***

On Christmas Eve, the family comes around. We have a simple meal together and exchange gifts. Or, rather, exchange 'gift' – we do a Kris

Kindle, whereby everyone present gets to both contribute and take one gift from a common pool (as opposed to having to buy a gift for everyone). I receive an artisan cup and saucer – a very beautiful piece that I still have today, handmade by a local craftswoman. I take out the guitar, and begin to sing. After singing 'Fairytale of New York' – probably the greatest Christmas song ever written – I manage to persuade my sister-in-law to grab her bassoon and join me for a jam. A mere week before, she had graduated college with a degree in music performance, with dreams of playing in the best symphonies on the continent. Now, here she is jamming old Pogues numbers with a drunken Irishman.

You took my dreams from me/ When I first found you.

When the family leaves in the early evening, Marie and I drive to Miller Hill Mall for a little last-minute shopping. We had already exchanged gifts back in Dublin before we left. We got a dog – a grand oul' thing that we got from a rescue shelter in Athy. We called her Suki. We could not, however, 'exchange' her on Christmas morning, due to the slight impracticality of transporting a gift-wrapped canine over the Atlantic. So we decided to set ourselves a rule. We would go to Miller Hill on Christmas Eve with $20 and an hour in which to spend it. By the end of the hour, we have to have a gift.

We go to bed that evening. At eight, we wake. We go downstairs and open our gifts. I get a George W. Bush quote-a-day calendar and a biography of former President Warren Harding from Marie. She gets edible underwear and a Bart Simpson lollipop. Well done, Seán. Still – it is Christmas, and we are all excited. The cover of my Warren Harding book carries his photo. I get everyone to pose, individually, with Harding's face for a photo.

We eat breakfast – waffles with whipped cream and cherries – and wash it down with lashings of creamy Egg Nog (with a dram of brandy to boot). The lawn outside, beneath the living room window, is covered with six inches of pristine, virgin snow. Marie and I, speaking for the six-year-olds that we left behind two decades previously, go outside and write 'Gertie Sucks' in twenty-foot high lettering. My sister-in-law is less than impressed with her gift, but it is all we can afford.

We jump into the car and head to Lake Superior – a brisk morning walk along the frozen shores of the downtown lake walk should be enough to ward off the -20°C cold that has been trying to conquer our skin.

When we arrive, we are surprised to see that we are not the only ones who sought refuge there. There are people out walking their dogs. There are people out exercising. And there are some people who are simply out – taking some respite from the onslaught of another Christmas morning.

We walk. The lake itself has not frozen this year. The edges of the lake (where we are) however, are to prove an exception to this. A thin layer of glassy ice now marks the skin of the surface wherever it touches land. The ice continues out for about 10 or 20 feet. Then the lake takes over.

About ten minutes into our stroll, I see something that I have not seen before. In the lake, not five feet from shore, live a large community of frantic ducks. They are swimming furiously in circles. What is this?

Marie, resident duck-expert, explains. Apparently, ducks do this on waters that are prone to freezing so that they'll have a patch of open water in which to hunt, clean and swim. Amazing. We stand silently, resting upon the barrier for about a quarter of an hour, watching the marvels of what is, for me, a hitherto undiscovered duck culture. It is a well-organised little community. Of the thirty or so ducks present, about twenty are in the water splashing about – refusing to let a little thing like arctic weather spoil their party. The remainder – ten or so – are at rest. Heavily. Whether true or not, I get the impression that they are shift workers, and have organised their labour into three distinct patterns – two in the water at any one time, the third group resting. It really is a sight to behold and makes me wonder (as almost everything does) why some humans try to make out that they are somehow not a part of the animal kingdom. Culture is, in human terms, the manner in which a problem is solved to the benefit of more than one individual. Is that not what I am seeing here with the ducks?

Soon, the cold gets the better of us. We leave the ducks to it and head home. We pass the rest of a very pleasant Christmas day by hanging out. Nothing more.

***

During my visits to America, I see the worst it has to offer. Poverty. Inequality. Racism. I have also seen much of the best America has to offer. People. Individuality. Self-confidence. I am now about to have a taste of wealthy America – see how 'the other half' lives. A friend of Marie's has invited us to their parents' lakeside cabin for New Years. 'Sounds great,' I think – a nice warm cabin offering a welcome refuge from the winter cold. Friendly glasses clinked together as the clock strikes 1 January. A quiet affair – not the kind of thing I am used to – but then, there's never enough variety on my spice-rack.

But first, we will start out by visiting the bar that Marie's dad had recently purchased – the Bedrock Bar in Duluth – which carries an excellent slogan – which, I must admit, I do not get at first: 'Your Day's Not Over Till You Make The Bedrock.' The Bedrock is a great little blue-collar bar in West Duluth – the kind of place that a person can go to have a drink, a game of pool or, in my case, a turn on the Karaoke machine, after a hard day. Marie and I have a fantastic time. We are supposed to stay only for an hour – from about 7.00 p.m. to 8.00 p.m. – but don't leave until after ten. The people are great. The musical entertainment – a Country 'n' Western group – are good. And the craic is ninety. We have already agreed to meet friends with whom to ring in the New Year – but I'm quite happy to stay here.

At about ten, we leave West Duluth, having spent a pleasant evening imbibing, and head out to Island Lake.

"Is there a lake in Island Lake?" I ask naively.

There comes no reply from the front of the car – only smiles.

As we drive down Rice Lake Road, Marie and Gertie sit in the front of the car, yammering on about supermodels and shoes, no doubt. I put my head back, and look at the sky. I have never seen one like it. It is like a fake sky set from an old 1950s Western movie. Big stars actually light the sky – which is itself framed on either side of the car by tall birch and pine trees, lightly frosted with snow.

Suddenly, a streak forces its way across the sky – a beautiful yellow-orange flash that has been travelling for a billion years, trying to make it here in time for me to see. Now, I have seen a very unusual amount of shooting stars in my time – I still see five or six a year. The star that I have seen tonight proves to be the most spectacular. I want to shout to Marie and Gertie to look – but I know that it will have passed by the time they can react. So I decide to say nothing. I just look at the sky, and wait for the streak to peter out.

But it does not do so immediately. Instead, I witness one of the most amazing sights Nature has yet offered me to consume. The streak swiftly and steadily becomes a thick fire-streak – smooth-edged tail sacrificed for ruffled ribbons. The fire turns a bright yellow.

I am in awe.

"Marie – Look – A Shooting Star!" But it is too late. It is gone.

"That's nice," comes the patronising reply.

I am not upset at this reaction. It means that this is one memory I get to keep all to myself. I keep my exhilarated eyes firmly fixed upon the impressionist sky for the remainder of the short trip. Soon, we pull into a driveway in a wooded area. A huge, beautiful wooden *house* stands before of me.

"*This* is a cabin?"

Turns out that, although technically a cabin, it has been built as the friend's parents' retirement house. We go inside. It is quite magnificent. Two reception areas. Offices. Bedrooms. Well-planned kitchen. I am impressed.

"Have a look out back."

I walk over to the sliding doors in the dining area and open them. There, before me, lies a breathtaking scene. The house has been built

overlooking Island Lake — literally. It even has its own jetty access to
the lake.

The evening is perfect. A few games. A few drinks. And when midnight
arrives? We all go out into the -20°C weather, slip into the seven-seater
hot-tub on the decking, overlooking the lake, and sip champagne. We do
not have a clock out there with us – but know that 2004 has arrived when
fireworks began to light up the already starlit night. In America, a little
wealth can be made to go a long way. Unfortunately for me, the same
cannot be said about a little money. The hot-tub bubbles finish at around
the same time as we drain the last of the champagne bubbles from our
glasses.

***

It's 2.00 p.m. on 2 January 2004. We are standing in the Check-in area of
Minneapolis-St Paul International Airport, waiting to catch the first of
three flights. Chicago. London. Dublin. Gertie drops us to the airport.
We check our bags.

It is not long before we realise something is wrong. There is an unusual
crowd of people at the airport – long queues. All of the TVs have been
switched to the weather channel. I overhear a conversation – "…flight
delays because of fog". Ah well, as long as it doesn't affect Chicago.

"Everywhere's clear except for Chicago."

Feck. I look at the weather map. Surely enough, almost the entire
continent of North America is clear – with the literal exception of a
localised fog patch affecting the area around Chicago-O'Hare. Great.
Well – not to worry. We are due to leave here at three. As long as we are
in the air by 5.30 p.m., we'll make our connection to Dublin.

"Chicago flights won't take off until six."

Feck.

We pass a long few hours watching the screens. The fog patch is
not lifting from the Chicago area. We are sitting with the Ladies US
Rugby team, who are equally as bored and anxious as we are. They are,

bizarrely, all dressed in their shorts — perhaps expecting a little mid-flight turbulence. I am struck by how young, short and far from muscular they look. A decent scrum in Chicago could well push them all back to Minneapolis.

After what seems a couple of lifetimes, we are off. It will, however, be a close-run thing. We are to fly Delta as far as Chicago and Aer Lingus the rest of the way. The flight is a little rocky. The turbulence outside is matched by the mild turbulence inside — we are sitting amongst the rugby squad who are, understandably, bored to the point of giddiness. Rugby ball substitutes and other unclassifiable projectiles hurtle now back and forth. The non-rugby playing contingent of passengers don't seem to mind, though.

I ask one of the Delta stewards if he thinks we will be on the ground in time to make our 7.30 p.m. Aer Lingus flight. To his credit, although he does not know, he asks each of the other stewards before having the pilot radio Chicago O'Hare to get an update. Even with this information, we will not know until we get there. It will be a close call.

At 6.50 p.m. the plane lands in the Windy City, or rather, at its airport. We de-plane, thank the crew for their efforts, and run.

By seven o'clock we have made it to the Aer Lingus gate. The plane is still there — but is readying for take-off. We have missed our flight. We watch in exhausted silence as the lumbering Jumbo Jet slowly reverses from the jetway and begins to make its way back to Ireland without us.

Looking around, we realise that we are not the only ones who have been affected by the fog. About thirty irate Irish people stand around in silence, anger and confusion as they watch their craft pull out onto the runway and take off. Why has the plane left without so many of them?

The Aer Lingus desk is in another Terminal. It takes us a good ten minutes to reach it using the airport's internal transit network. It is a scene of lawlessness. Throngs of irate, red-faced (hairy) Irishmen are in line looking for a fight. The red face of one such missing link approaches me.

"That's all bullshit about the fog. There is no fog."

"Oh?" I venture, knowing otherwise.

"It's all a poxy cover-up."

I am not sure why he thinks that the airline figure it a good idea to leave us all behind – or why he is so important or infamous to cause one of the world's biggest airlines to plot against him. I won't dwell on it, though.

We are all in line – about forty or so of us. Aer Lingus completely mismanage the situation.

"We're only contractors – we can't do anything for you," shouts one over and over, like a parrot with obsessive-compulsive disorder.

"Go to American Airlines – they'll help you," shouts another – repeatedly.

One rep is actually talking with the customers – but amazingly is only dealing with those who are shouting the loudest! The queue system has broken down.

After my conspiracy friend gives the customer service agent an earful for lying about the fog, assassinating Kennedy and trying to pollute his precious bodily fluids (despite the fact that he was behind me in the line) I manage to stop her. I put my tickets into her hand and ask her why I should go to the American desk – I am flying with Delta.

"Go to the American desk," she instructs me, waving my tickets back at me.

We follow her orders. Three hours later (I am not kidding), we reach the head of the line for the American desk. It is late – almost midnight. I am tired, in need of a shower. Most of all – I want to know how I am going to get home.

I explain my situation to the girl behind the counter. I show her my tickets.

"I don't know why they sent you here. You need to talk to either Delta or Aer Lingus. There's nothing we can do for you."

Marie cries. I feel empty.

We trudge back to the Aer Lingus desk. Not only is it closed – a sign indicates that it will be closed until at least 4.00 p.m. the next day.

I find a payphone and call the 24-hour Aer Lingus Customer Service help-line. Closed for the night. Great. The twenty-four hours must be non-consecutive.

We locate the Delta desk on an airport map and decide to give it one more go. We make our way to yet another floor of yet another Terminal. It is deserted. The Delta lights are out. I am just about to give up when Marie notices something – a Delta worker.

We approach and frantically tell the fifty-something black woman our story. She is to become not only my saviour, but my favourite American. She smiles, and calms us down. She cannot understand why neither of the two previous airlines would help us – apparently they all have access to the same systems.

She tells us to come back the next day and talk to Aer Lingus – they might be able to get us on a flight. If not, as a back-up plan, she books us onto a flight that would get us home – through Copenhagen, and three days late, on Tuesday morning. But it is something concrete, despite the fact that my exams for a Graduate Diploma in Business Studies are due to start on Tuesday morning. (I have been studying all throughout my trip). She gives us a discount voucher for an airport hotel and a number to call. We have somewhere to stay for the night. I like this woman. I even sent an email to Delta about her. She had guaranteed us a night's sleep – which we will, no doubt, badly need.

A quick phone call and the booking is made. Soon, we are on the hotel shuttle bus and on our way.

I cannot remember the name of the hotel. It is a chain, however – about the equivalent of a two-star. But comfortable. And clean. As we unlock the door to our room – and fall inside – something dawns upon us. Quickest case scenario: we leave Chicago tomorrow evening. That means we have extended our trip by one day, and have a new city to explore. In a sense, it is a free holiday – or, at least, sanity dictates that we treat it as such.

I make a quick trip to the lobby to see if I can get any info on Chicago tourism. All I manage to find is a leaflet for The Field Museum. It houses the largest, most complete T Rex yet found (named 'Sue').

'Sounds OK,' we think.

By morning, we have read the leaflet – our only piece of reading material – about twenty times each. The excessive tiredness and limited reading material take their toll. Our conversations now go something like this:

"Just think – the biggest T-Rex in the world! In the whole wide world!"

"Yeah – I know. It's going to be brilliant."

"She's four times the height of a man."

"I'd hate to get caught in her teeth."

"If we stuff our breakfast down our throats, we'll be able to go sooner."

"Yeah. Great."

***

The friendly, non-English speaking driver of the airport shuttle drops us off at the airport light rail station. We will take the train into downtown Chicago. When we get to the station, we are not sure exactly where to go. I stop an employee – mid-fifties, grey hair – and ask.

"You Irish?" he asks.

"Er, yep."

"I'm Irish too."

Great. Here we go again. I had decided that if in this situation again I would let the other party divulge the information they want to share, and get it over with. I never know what line of questioning to use to feign interest: the 'Really – which part?' response usually leads to embarrassment, since the Irish part is located in the testicle or ovary of an ancestor. That, or they answer 'London' or something, before telling me how it is all the same, since we have the same Queen. No matter how often I hear it, it is always fresh news to me.

My silence works. He picks up the conversation.

"Yeah – I was born on the Falls Road, Belfast."

Well feck me. He actually is Irish – and what is even more amazing – he was born in the *same part of Belfast* as my grandmother. We have a little conversation – or, rather, he has a little monologue, during which he manages to return to the Falls. If only I had that power last night.

We leave him behind – as does he – and find our platform. Soon, we are on our way. The light rail goes through a bit of a tunnel and emerges into the Illinois daylight. The track runs down the median of the highway all the way to the city rim – a great idea that should be taken up elsewhere. Giant, drab cars race past the train. Marie's father had told her about Chicago traffic – all bumper-to-bumper, all 80 miles an hour. It is true. It seems that here, the big car is less a phallic symbol than a muscular necessity needed to push one's way into and out of the traffic.

Twenty minutes later we are elevated, and travelling above the streets. It looks remarkably like the surviving late-Victorian part of Dublin. All around me, I see people on their way to work, on their way to class, on their way to shop. There are people who have no 'way' to be on and spend their days allowing the rail to dictate where they go. There are smiling people who look as if they haven't a care in the world, and people who look as if they do nothing but worry. And I – the accidental *voyageur* – sitting amongst them.

The train enters another tunnel. Looks like our stop will be underground. Two stops later, and we get off at (what is, hopefully) the right stop. We follow the signs to street level, and alight.

Downtown Chicago. *Wow*. What a city. I am instantly mesmerised. It is tall. It is elegant. It is beautiful. The sky sits neatly upon the massive skyscrapers – all of which glow warmly in the cold January morning. Here I am in Chicago – one of the greatest cities on earth.

We wander around in awe for a few minutes – walking along, enjoying the visual aesthetic effervescence, soaking it all in. It is a pretty, pretty city.

We decide to catch the bus out to Museum Campus and see the T-Rex – Sue – the one who kept us up all night, the one who worked us into a delirium. We make our way to a bus stop, and wait. Within five minutes, we are on our way. The bus journey is equally pleasant. We drive past the John Hancock Centre. The waterfront. It is beautiful. Soon, we are at Museum Campus. We leave the bus and enter the cold of a windy January morning.

The Field Museum is having a rare free day. No fee. Nice timing. No sooner do we enter than we see her. There, standing in full splendour, is Sue, the largest known specimen of a T-Rex. I am…not as impressed as I had anticipated.

Now, I know a thing or two about your common T-Rex. I grew up with them, despite the minor matter of them having been extinct for tens of millions of years. I watched them as they guested on numerous cartoons and TV specials. They are in movies. They are in books. They are, by all accounts, fearsome creatures, known to level entire Japanese cities on their worse days. They are creatures that don't like being kept in theme parks. They are wild. They are king – as the name *Rex* implies.

And yet, here is the biggest of them. Sue. She looks short. And, what's more, she doesn't look like the kind of creature that would terrify residents of Tokyo so much that they speak with their lips and words out of synch. And as for theme parks – she could easily fit into the orang-utan enclosure at Dublin Zoo. She'd be cramped, but she'd fit.

I find it…refreshing, I must say. It seems to me that the legend makers have gotten it wrong. Here stands a nonetheless magnificent creature that looks more a scavenger on the margins of a dinosaur society than king. The legends – though fascinating – don't seem to hold true. The Spielbergian monster – the Terror of Tokyo – the marketers' dream – is a creature of myth. Sue wouldn't be more than an appetiser for one of Spielberg's lads. Looks like the DNA he used is a bit dodgy – and the bad disposition of his monster can probably be explained by the fact that it was cloned to be too big to feed properly. But don't let the facts stop people believing the story – the legend has a potency all of its own.

We spend another three or so hours exploring the museum. This is due in no small part to the realisation that we are down to our last $18 and might have to spend a few days here. The museum is, itself, a very interesting place – a sort of generic museum with exhibits from almost every field of interest one can imagine – palaeontology, anthropology, history, etc. It is also an excellent place to do some research into 'Americanology' – the study of Americans. Because of its broad subject matter and its specific attractions, such as Sue, it attracts a large patronage. In the canteen area, we sit awhile watching in silence as the locals pass by – not a tourist in sight – except for the one I encounter in the bathroom mirror. Damn Irish!

This extensive observational fieldwork research into Americanology lends further credence to my assertion that American people are no different to Europeans, at the heart of it. They are as intrigued by *things* as others. They are as family-oriented as anyone else. The only real difference is in how they dress to go to these places, and how they tell their friends about what they've seen.

It is approaching 3.00 p.m. – time to go and try the Aer Lingus desk one more time. We leave the museum and make our way into the middle of the crowded Museum Campus. A friendly looking black man approaches me – fiftyish, smiling.

"Here's a gift for you from Chicago," he says, as he places a Chicago postcard into my hands.

"Oh – er, thanks," I respond, not really sure why the city has chosen me to bestow a gift upon. I am, after all, an accidental traveller. I guess that the city must be a little desperate for heroes – something that I do not really consider myself. Sure, I have overcome adversity to turn a potentially devastating and life-changing event like missing a flight into nothing more than a pleasant day in Chicago, but to call me a *hero*?

I wake from my daydreaming to find the man still standing there, smiling, and looking for me to do something. Hmm. A photo-op, perhaps, for the local press? *'Irish Hero Sets Example to Stranded Travellers Everywhere'*.

Marie interrupts my delusions of grandeur.

"You're supposed to give him something for it."

"Oh – sure. OK," I say, reaching into my pocket. I produce $3.

"Here," I sputter, handing over a fisted bunch of crumple.

"Thank you," and he is gone.

Turns out that I am not a hero – or, at least, not the kind I build myself up to be. I am a hero in the sense that I buy a 10¢ postcard for $3 and have, inadvertently, made a donation to a local unemployment charity. It might not mean a photo-op, however – still, at least I know what I am.

"What did you buy that for?" asks Marie, knowing that we are down to $15 – a mere $4 off the $11-a-day threshold for defining poverty, according to the UN.

"Er, I knew I would be helping a charity," I lie.

We are getting hungry. No matter what it is converted into, $15 rarely looks appetising. I am afraid that we'll soon have to eat the postcard. It is Sue that gives me this idea – after all, she ate Tokyo. I will only be eating *a picture* of a city. But I soon get turned off the idea. If it was New York, it would be a much easier prospect. I would simply close my eyes, take a mouthful of postcard, and picture a big apple. But Chicago? The Windy City? I can't do that to Marie – not with the prospect of ten hours flying in an enclosed steel tube. She'll have to endure the flight breathing the farts of hundreds of other passengers as it is: I'll give her a break and leave the postcard as the last culinary option.

Despite the cold, we saunter back to the light rail station, soaking up Chicago. Soon, we are back on the train, making our way back to the latest of my nemeses to thwart me – Chicago O'Hare. *Damn big airports.*

We approach the Aer Lingus desk – we are the only passengers there. We calmly explain our dilemma and wait to hear the worst – not only could we not fly, but the airline has managed to pin both the Lincoln and McKinley assassinations on me or something. But it doesn't happen.

"Oh, sure. You can fly tonight. Now, we can't actually guarantee it until about an hour before departure, but it should be fine."

What? This is a large airport, isn't it? This is the same airport that had conspired against me as recently as yesterday, isn't it? What is going on? We are issued boarding passes. In four hours, we'll know our fate.

We decide to pin all of our hopes on this, and find a food court to eat. We order a pizza – when in Rome, do as the Romans do. When in Chicago, eat pizza. Until this trip, I never fully understood that saying. We have surprisingly good airport pizza. When finished, we have three hours to kill. Might as well go to the gates.

What we don't yet know is that the US government have raised the terrorist alert to – well, actually I'm not sure. I never quite get their colour system. I presume that 'orange' is the highest level of terror alert since they dress their Afghan prisoners in that colour. 'Green' is an IRA threat, 'red' indicates an imminent Communist plot and a 'pink' alert means that the country is under imminent threat of gay people marrying. The terror threat means that it will take a little longer to clear the security area. It usually takes about twenty minutes. With this delay, we expect it to double. We join the queue.

Just over two hours later, we clear it – not before I have been frisked by some guy in uniform that I hope is an employee, and my shoes have been searched on two separate occasions.

We make our way to our gate. The Aer Lingus plane is there at the end of the jetway. The plane slowly boards. As the seats in the Departure lounge clear of passengers, we become ever more nervous. Soon, we are the only people who have not boarded.

"Passengers Carabini and Skelton?"

Yes. We made it. We take our seats. Soon, the mighty engines rumble, and we leave America once again.

***

The airline food is dreadful, as usual. But it turns out that I probably could have eaten the postcard anyway. I am, in the end (probably due to the pizza) highly flatulent for the *entire* journey home. I'm not sure if Marie is technically asleep or not – but she is unconscious for most of the journey. Illinois. Michigan. Ontario. Quebec. Newfoundland. I sully the airspace of each in turn.

At nine o'clock in the morning, the plane touches down in grey Dublin and, in a quirky cultural habit that I've never encountered in any other country, but one that always happens in Dublin, the passengers applaud the crew. It always brings a smile to my face. We are back – with a mere 36 hours to spare before my exams begin. With this kind of pressure, a guy could really use a holiday.

CHAPTER NINE

Ticks and the Places They Hide

It would be a mere six months before we returned to the good ol' USA. For us, it proves an eventful six months. I end up passing the exams and getting my H-Dip in Business Studies. I also end up being diagnosed with Multiple Sclerosis. Feck. One 'sclero' is bad enough – but Multiple Sclerosis? Turns out that the type I have really isn't as bad as I had feared. All it amounts to is a kick up the arse for me to get my lifestyle in order. I'm now a bit of a health-freak – but not without reason.

However, the Multiple Sclerosis does introduce a new dynamic into our travel arrangements. My medication consists of three injections of a drug called Rebif every week. The syringes are pre-filled and temperature sensitive, meaning that, when we decide to fly anywhere, I must take my supply of syringes on board with me. Great. I have given my old large airport nemesis a new weapon to use against me.

We are to return to Minnesota in June – coinciding with our second anniversary, as it happens. The flight this time will follow yet another route. Our port of entry into the US will actually be Minneapolis, rather than Chicago or New York. We will first fly to London, where we are to connect with an Icelandair flight to Reykjavik. From there, it will be a straight flight to Minneapolis.

I have all of my medication passports, along with letters from my doctors and from the drug company. My medication is packed into a little purpose-made travel bag, complete with freezer pack to ensure that the contents will never be exposed to temperatures over 25°C. When diagnosed, I was given a choice of three different drugs to treat my condition. Since all of the drugs have a similar efficacy rate – about 30 per cent – the doctors left it up to me to choose a treatment. When my neurologist asked why I chose Rebif, I spouted off some nonsense about good results in clinical trials and excellent reputation. What I didn't tell him was the truth – I chose Rebif based on one sole consideration, the fact that it comes with a snazzy travel bag. It's fickle, but true.

Our first flight is with BMI. They want to know exactly what is in the bag, why I need to bring it on board. They thoroughly inspect the documentation. In fact, the Captain even requests to see the documentation himself. 'Fair enough, 'I think – 'after all, I am taking a potential weapon on board.' I wouldn't have expected them to be any less vigilant. In fact, I even kind of admire their thoroughness.

Within an hour, we are back in Heathrow and manage, again, to make it out of the 'backstage' area, entering the Check-in area without negotiating Immigration. Great. Heathrow strikes again.

Soon, we have checked in with Icelandair, and make our way to the gate. I was told by the woman at the Check-in area to let them know as I board that I have the syringes.

After a short wait, we begin to board. As I enter the craft, I step to the side and explain my syringe dilemma to a stewardess.

"So?" comes the reply.

I am a little thrown.

"Er, I just thought you needed to know."

"Er, no. Is there something you need me to do with them?"

"No."

"OK then. Welcome onboard."

I am confused. Why is there not the same fuss on Icelandair as there had – rightly – been on BMI? No request for documentation or explanation.

The craft speeds its way down the runway, lifting smoothly from the tarmac. The flight is…a different one. Usually, we have one or two short flights combined with a long flight, on which we can, at least, sleep. Travelling through Iceland does not afford this luxury. The London to Reykjavik leg takes a bit over four hours. The Reykjavik to Minneapolis leg takes about the same. I don't like this prospect. Too long to be a short flight and too short to be a long flight.

After about three or so hours, we reach the eastern Icelandic coast. About an hour's flight to the western coast before we land. This means an hour of aerial sightseeing. Iceland is stunning from the air. The entire island looks as if poured into the ocean. The land ripples and waves. It is sparse. It is bleak. It is beautiful. It has always been on my to-do list (visiting, that is) but, so far, this would be my only encounter with it. An enchanting hour later and we land.

The airport is in an unusually bleak location. It is surrounded by beautiful desolation and mountainous, looming horizons. A weed that I have never before seen abounds, turning the waste ground surrounding the runway into an endless purple carpet. Stunning.

The plane taxis to the only manmade structure in sight — a black box of a building that, as it turns out, is the main (and only) Terminal. We deplane, and enter the building. It is breathtakingly modern — as if designed by John Rocha himself. Elegant, black marble. Polished wood. Local igneous stone. The airport needs only a pair of legs to justify what would be a memorable, if slightly frightening, promenade down the catwalk.

We have noticed that the craft in which we have flown is one of only two in the entire airport. It isn't the busiest airport in the world, nor is it the biggest — but the locals don't seem to realise this. We find a screen that informs us of our next departure gate. Gate 54. We arrived at Gate 42. We also notice from the screen that there are only about ten or twelve flights all day expected at the airport. Gate 54? Still, ten out of ten for forward planning, I guess.

We find an on-site snack shop to see what we can pick up. Hmm… The choices are…interesting. Dried fish jerky, a dried fish chew, dried sea food sticks, and plain old dried fish. Realising that most of the fish on hand is the now-endangered cod, we decide to take a pass. Instead, we find a tiny sandwich bar and purchase a sandwich. Not knowing the lingo, we are not exactly sure what it is we are buying. It is for Marie, as I am now on a special wheat-free Multiple Sclerosis-busting diet. As Marie is a vegetarian, we are taking a bit of a risk. It turns out to be a dried fish sandwich. We should have known.

After an interminable though short wait, it is time to queue for the second leg. There are, by now, three planes ready to begin embarkation and leave for the USA. We are in the Minneapolis queue. There is also a Boston queue and a Seattle queue. The Bostonians are impeccably dressed – they all have come dressed to match the airport. They wear blacks and greys, and have accessorised perfectly. They look affluent – even if they aren't. The Seattleites have gone for a less monochrome palate, but one that is equally fashionable. All match their colourful luggage. Then there is the Mid-Western line – the Minnesotans. There are three major style setting areas in the USA – the New England area, including New York and Boston, the Pacific coast, including California and Seattle, and the South – the Cowboy style that epitomises rural America. The Mid-West is a net style consumer – unlike the style setting areas here listed. The problem is that it doesn't know which area to look to for guidance. A woman in front of me wears a faded yellow T-shirt with stonewashed jeans. A man behind me sports a mullet and a cowboy necktie. It is all wrong.

It is possible to locate someone geographically in the USA merely by looking at what they wear.

Woman: black skirt; black and grey check coat; black shoes; Ray-Ban sunglasses – she joins the Boston line.

Student: green combats; fashionable 'Elvis' T-shirt; nice blue sneakers; long, fashionably unkempt hair – she joins the Seattle line.

Woman: dyed hair, roots showing; mullet (an unkempt one at that); white jeans that give hints of thinner days and more than a hint of body parts; lumberjack shirt (no, *padded* lumberjack shirt) – she joins our line.

I must stress that I mean no offence to Mid-Westerners. With at least three distinctive fashion areas to choose from, and being of Germanic stock, where the links between fashion and Protestantism are revealed to their fullest – it's difficult to get it right. In an ironic way, this has actually given rise to a unique Mid-Western style which proves that while style may go out of fashion, fashion never goes out of style.

Soon, we board, with the same apathy towards my syringes that had been displayed in London. I am on my way once again to the American heartland, complete with the pink sunglasses and faux-fur-lined cord jacket with which I fully expect to make the local Best Dressed lists during my stay.

***

At 8.00 p.m. we arrive in Minneapolis-St Paul International Airport. Marie's sisters are there to greet us. Pleasantries out of the way, we make for the parking lot. *Wow*. The heat is crushing. It is evening time, but still over the 100°F mark. Pretty unbelievable stuff. Marie and I, tired from the trip, fall into the back of the car, and from there, quickly pass somnambulism into a deep, deep sleep. Gertie points the car towards Duluth, and off we go.

I wake as the car passes over the crest of the hills overlooking Duluth. The night-time city lights glow beautifully below us – always a stunning sight, no matter how often I see it. Soon, we are in Lakewood, the area of Duluth where we usually stay, and in bed.

Each trip to the USA has had its theme. There was the Christmas trip. There was the Army Worm/Wedding trip. This would be the Wildlife trip.

As it turns out, with the exception of the bobcat, I haven't really seen that much of American wildlife. I had been in Minnesota in June before, but did not see any typical June creatures – the Army Worms last time had affected the ecosystem to such a degree that insects which would normally compete for the same foods could not. The food chain was adversely affected, all the way up to the red-necks who, by my estimation, probably died in their thousands due to the depletion of the squirrel population.

The next morning, Marie and I wake by nine. We get dressed, and go outside for a stroll through the surrounding birch woods. I am wearing sandals – my first pair, I must admit. Don't get much use for them in damp ol' Ireland. We stomp our way through the Army Worm-free woods – chatting and relaxing. After twenty or so minutes, we return to the house.

"Right," says Marie. "Tick check."

What?

"What do you mean?"

"Check yourself for ticks."

"Er, what is a tick?" I ask naively.

"A tick – you know – those little bugs that bury their heads into your skin and suck your blood."

There is silence.

"What??!!"

It soon dawns upon Marie that I am a tick virgin. She gives me a tutorial on ticks and their ways. Here's what I learn in Tick Check 101. There are two different types of ticks – the regular kind, about a quarter of the size of a fingernail, and Deer ticks, which are about the size of this full-stop. Regular ticks are brownish-red in colour. Once on the skin, they slowly lumber across the vast plains and through the mighty crevasses of the body until they find a nice warm secluded spot – like a groin or an armpit. That's when they tuck in – literally. They sink their heads through the skin into the bloodstream and drink until they are about the size and colour of a repulsive little grape. If found, it is not advisable to simply pull them off – they have developed an ingenious self-defence mechanism. In the shock, they tend to vomit their contents directly back into the bloodstream – something the body generally frowns upon. There is another danger to this gung-ho 'George W. Bush' school of thought to tick removal – while one might be successful in pulling their full little bodies out, the head might detach. This can lead to a nasty skin and blood infection, which is fine until that pretty girl sitting next to you on the bus asks why you look a little under the weather, and you have to tell her that not only do ticks burrow into you, but that if she looks real close, she can still see their heads.

Great. Regular ticks – being much bigger than the Deer ticks – are obviously the worse of the two, the ones to keep an eye out for, right? Well, actually, no. Deer ticks are harder to spot, which is particularly bad, since they are known to carry Lyme disease – a nasty condition that, depending on the publication you read, causes anything from a type of arthritis to a condition that will eat your brain. Score!

Now that I have the basics, I need to learn how to conduct a tick check. No problem. Just a matter of looking down into your T-shirt and double-checking any place that itches, right? Again, no. Because ticks are such slow things, they're hard to spot. A tick check is like a mole check crossed with a proctology exam. I duly carry out the tick check using a wall mirror, a bathroom cabinet, an angled lamp and a good sense of balance. Throw into this a little forensics, as each and every seam of clothing must be checked to make sure they're not hiding.

The ticks are not everywhere, I am relieved to hear. As a general rule, they are only in wooded areas and in areas of long grass. That means two weeks of hanging out in the middle of a freshly cut lawn.

I finish my cautious tick check just in time to hear Marie calling me from the downstairs bathroom.

"Look," she says, pointing to her exposed stomach. "That's a tick."

Sure enough, the little raisin that wanted to be a grape lumbers slowly along. Marie introduces him to tweezers, and brings him outside while I breathe into a paper bag.

The next day, we take a trip to Gordon, Wisconsin, to see the house on the St Croix River that Marie's mother is building for herself. It is a beautiful spot – secluded, wooded, rural. We pull into the driveway, and deplane. Sorry – I mean get out of the car. The first thing I notice is that the red dirt driveway is pock-marked. Ants. An insect that I know. An insect that I fear. And they are here in their millions. Feck.

My loathing of ants comes not from the fact of their insect state, but their intelligence. They build cities based on a division of labour so efficient that it brings into question the very idea that we are the top species around here. They farm. They hunt. They are *brutal* in their efficiency. And that's where my fear is seated. I don't trust anything that I can't outsmart or predict. That, and the abiding memory of camping in Ireland next to a hill full of winged, flying, scary-as-shit ants in the Wicklow Mountains as a teenager.

But I digress. The house is, as previously mentioned, a stone's throw from the St Croix River – which we duly follow a short track to reach. An old logging dam runs across a tributary of the St Croix at the foot of the slope upon which the house is being constructed. We cautiously cross it to an island in the middle of the river. The dam is little more than a ramshackle – if very efficient – collection of stones, logs, mud and tall grasses. We cross over, and cross back. It is very rewarding – particularly in the 80°F plus heat.

As we return to the building site, a thought crosses my mind. 'Tall grasses? Wooded area? June?' I race back to the building site, hoping to be first into the bathroom. Turns out that I am about four months too early.

"The bathroom?" I enquire.

A grin and a pointed finger reveal an outhouse. Great. In another trick from Mother Nature, a chicken is revealed to everyone present, as I refuse to enter the outhouse. Why swap a known entity, like a tick, for something unknown, like a bear? Possible?

I watch the National Geographic channel. I know that the tourist is usually the first to get eaten. Well, him or the sea captain. And we are 2000 miles from the open sea.

I do the best preliminary check I can. I look down into my T-shirt. No ticks.

"Seán – come and see!" calls Marie.

She again exposes her stomach, and points to a full stop. There being no sentence in front of it, I think I know what she is trying to tell me.

"See? That's a Deer tick."

With that (and, amazingly, a smile), she takes tweezers, and plucks off the tick. What the hell have I married?

I am getting a bit antsy (literally) and feeling crawlier than I usually do.

Thus, I manage to hurry everyone else up. Soon, we are on the way back to some sort of civilisation. When we arrive back, I commandeer the bathroom on the main floor, and check every square inch of skin and clothing I can find – no matter who it belongs to. Turns out that I am being too broad. I should have checked every millimetre.

It is night-time. I sit on the bed, undressing. Marie is downstairs brushing her teeth. I take off my T-shirt. One last look. No tick. I proceed to remove my jeans. Instant horror. Frozen. Panic. There, crawling drowsily along the inside of my right thigh is Lucifer himself – in tick form.

My reaction is…less than heroic. I scream. And I scream. And then, just for good measure, I scream some more. Soon, my screams begin to mingle with words – I now scream for Marie. I also do the one thing that I shouldn't do with a tick when going to bed. I flick him – alive – onto the carpet.

Marie comes into the room. I am, by now, heroically cowering beneath the blankets, being mentally eaten alive by Satan's tiny minions.

"What's wrong?"

"A tick."

"Oh. Where?" she asks calmly.

"Er, there," I say, pointing to the ground. "I flicked him onto the carpet."

"You flicked him onto the carpet? Why do you flick him onto the carpet? You should have thrown him outside!"

"You want me to touch him? He could burrow into my fingers if I tried that! And then where would we be? Do you want me to lose a finger? Is that your little fetish?"

Marie soon realises that I am not really kidding. The drama queen in me is giving one of her spontaneous, unpredictable, Oscar-winning performances. Luckily, the carpet is a shag pile carpet. All we have to do is stare. Sure enough, like tall grasses parted by a lion in the Serengeti, the piles are shagging slowly left and right. The tick! I suddenly know how Captain Ahab must have felt near the end. Not having a harpoon and, momentarily, not having any balls, I resort to using a combination of tweezers and Marie to rid myself of the demon tick. She takes him (or her) downstairs and flings him/her back into the woods. Some say that he's there still – lying in wait to attach himself to unsuspecting out-of-towners. Nobody knows for sure, though. What is true, however, is that Marie and I are the only two to have seen him and lived to tell the tale of the Demon Tick from Hell.

***

On this trip, I am determined to do many of the tourist attractions that I have not yet gotten around to doing. And by this, I don't mean the obvious attractions – I have already 'done' the Mall of America, for example. Instead, I want to see the individual, unique roadside attractions that Minnesota has to offer. I previously mentioned the fact that America is a country in which everyone can potentially contribute to the culture – I want to see what this State has thrown into that mix. And so, one beautiful sunny morning, we set out for the sprawling metropolis that is Grand Rapids, Minnesota.

There are obvious tourist destinations – God knows America's full of them. They include the Grand Canyon, Disneyland and the Statue of Liberty. And then there are those which are not so obvious – those that take a leap of faith. It is these I find most rewarding – mini-pilgrimages where the sheer crassness of the attraction and the odd notion that one has gone out of one's way to visit it is, in itself, half the fun. America is full of great attractions for people who want to stray from the beaten path. Today would be one such day for me, for we are going to see the Judy Garland Birthplace in Grand Rapids, Minnesota.

Duluth to Grand Rapids is a good two-hour drive. I see from the map that most of the drive would be through Indian country – the Fond Du Lac reservation. Great. I've never seen a reservation before. I am not necessarily expecting to see a scene from *Dances With Wolves*. I am not even expecting to see that much from the car. But I am expecting at least *some* difference. There is, however, to be none. The car drives through the reservation on a regular looking highway. The houses we pass would not have looked out of place in suburban Minneapolis. They even have Star-Spangled Banners apole in their gardens. I begin to wonder if the only reason for the existence of the reservation is to prevent the full absorption of these people into American culture so that they will, like everyone else in America, have a non-American homeland with which to identify themselves and their heritage.

But I digress.

At about 2.00 p.m., we arrive in Grand Rapids – a town masquerading as a city. More 'mini-apolis' than Minneapolis. But pleasant enough, with well-kept houses, streets, schools and even a lake or two.

Pretty soon, we begin to see signs for the Birthplace. We follow them (twice – we get lost the first time) down a busy highway that has been sullied with ugly strip malls and their inevitably loud signs. And, suddenly, at a crossroads, there it is. Looks a little out of place – but no matter.

In we go, and find the ultimate Judy Garland museum. We follow exhibits that unfold her life chronologically. The story is occasionally interspersed with personal items and movie props, including the horse-drawn carriage from the Emerald city in *The Wizard of Oz*. The carriage was, oddly enough, once owned by Abraham Lincoln – a fact which should come in handy for the more adventurous players of the game 'Six Degrees of Kevin Bacon'. At the end of the exhibit is an area where it is possible to sit and watch a constantly running documentary about Judy. I stop awhile.

The documentary is dealing with what is, arguably, the greatest performance of her last few years – the singing of the 'Battle Hymn of the Republic' live on her own TV programme in 1963, following the assassination of JFK. I have never seen the piece before but can honestly say that it is one of the best musical performances that I have seen. The hairs stand on the back of my neck, and, for a moment, I know what it is like to feel American-style patriotism in my blood.

The museum adjoins the house, linked by a corridor which displays the *pièce de résistance* – the ruby slippers themselves. Apparently, there is more than one pair – each valued (if memory serves me correctly) at around $3 million. However, I can report that at the time of writing, the slippers are missing, stolen – the small town USA equivalent of New York losing Lady Liberty. The police have no leads, but Kansas might be a good place to start looking.

From there, we enter the house itself. It is quite interesting from a historical perspective – it is, essentially, a preserved time capsule of the period – turn of the 20th-century middle class USA. Museums of this sort always fascinate me. For all of our supposed sophistication, we essentially aspire to the same lifestyle now and want the same things as they did then – the only difference being that we want our things to plug in.

It takes just a little over an hour to *do* the museum, but I thoroughly enjoy it. After all, I had set out to enjoy it. We are just about to head back to Duluth when we notice an advert in one of the innumerable tourist magazines I pick up. It is for Itasca National Park – the headwaters of the mighty Mississippi – and it is, according to the advert, just one short hour away. That's where we will go.

An hour later, we are still an hour away. So we decide – or, rather, I decide – that we should take a short cut by leaving the highway and using some of the smaller, clearer county roads. It turns out to be a good move.

I sit in the back of the car, gazing out into the dense forests beside us, thinking of what could be in there: Sasquatch? Mountain Lions? Moose?

"Bear!" shouts Gertie.

Yes. And bear.

"Look!"

Before I have time to think, I see it. Although we are travelling quite fast, all happens in slow motion. And it is simple too. From the woods to the right of the car emerges a black bear. The animal puts its nose in the air and sniffs around a bit. And then it is gone. It is a pretty magnificent sight. I have finally seen a bear. I am tempted to feed it doughnuts and get Marie to take my picture – something that I, not being raised here, had missed out on doing as a child. But not to worry.

Having never seen a black bear (or any wild bear) before, it is a great thrill. It is interesting to see how small the bear is – it looks only about the size of a large dog, but its girth is that of about three Rottweilers stapled together. Its fur seems shaggier than I would have expected – probably due to the excessive June temperatures – shaggy and brown – distinctly brown – as opposed to black. The bear behaviourist in me surmises that it is probably either out looking for a feed or trying to find the Judy Garland museum. Hmm…I wonder if it is the same bear in rabbit's clothing that tried to eat me in the hot tub the Christmas before?

Soon, we reach the gates of Itasca. We enter, and follow a road to the parking lot. A small brook piddles its way along the road's edge to the right. We passed a sign. The name of the brook? The mighty Mississippi. Now this is impressive – like a child called Zeus or Thor – the promise of the tiny stream disproportionate to its great name, as if it is proclaiming to the world 'Here I am! I am the Mighty Mississippi!'…in falsetto. It is…sweet.

We park the car and follow a trail that leads down to the headwaters themselves. And there it is. An absolutely idyllic setting. Lake Itasca – a lake large enough by European standards – surrounded by woods, spills out over rocks that look like a small, submerged causeway. On one side of the rocks is the lake. On the other is the Mississippi. I remove my shoes and socks and walk – cautiously – across the rocks – momentarily becoming part of the source of this mightiest of rivers. I am one of many to partake in this tradition. I then walk back through the Mississippi itself – the refreshingly cool, clear waters combine beautifully with the hot, dry evening. There's the inevitable sense of awe that all visitors feel as they try to comprehend the river itself, flowing on south for literally *thousands* of miles until it reaches the Gulf of Mexico just past New Orleans. It's a mythical river – *the* American river, as important to the national soul as the Grand Canyon or New York City. The story of

America cannot be told without the Mississippi. And here I am walking across the headwaters – a fitting monument in a serene location that allows one to contemplate the myth – a rare myth that it is possible to see, to feel and, today, to walk across. It is a symbol of the American spirit – Itasca reminds Americans (and it is more or less only Americans that visit) that all great things have a small beginning. From here, in this quiet, beautiful corner of Minnesota, it seems obvious that the river *is* the dream.

We decide to go for a walk around the rest of the park – or some of it at any rate. I am thinking of Henry Schoolcraft – the 19th-century explorer who discovered the source of the river. I managed to talk Marie, her sister and her mom into coming here today. To my relief, they are enjoying the experience and also contemplating the significance. I myself feel a weird sense of privilege at seeing this place. What must Schoolcraft have felt when he realised what he had found? What must he have thought when he uncovered the Mississippi, spilling so gently over the rocky lip of Lake Itasca?

And then I see a sign. It is a sign that explains the history of the location. Turns out that Schoolcraft did not see what I saw today. What he saw was a swampy, marshy area, complete with swarming mosquitoes. Rather than spill gently from the lake, the river oozed its way out of a marsh. The source of the great river was more or less indistinguishable.

Enter Franklin Delano Roosevelt, the great President of the Depression era. As part of his plan to bring jobs to the people, he started the massive Public Works Administration. One of the many, many projects envisaged as part of that scheme was to give the Mississippi a definable source – to give the great river a more fitting start in life. Thus, the stones are not original. The definite connection of the river and the lake is not original. This idyll has been engineered – albeit beautifully so. To paraphrase the line from John Ford's *The Man Who Shot Liberty Valance*: 'This is the (Mid-) West, Sir. When the legend becomes fact, print the legend.'

So what have I seen today? A Judy Garland birthplace that, although the original house, has long since moved from its original location. And the headwaters of the Mississippi – changed to fit a legend. This is something very American. If something is not quite the way you feel it should be, fix it. It is, in one sense, a quite wonderful part of the American psyche – a part that has caused America to invent, discover and engineer. The museum and the headwaters are two prime, if small scale, examples of this wonderful can-do spirit. This spirit got Americans to the Moon. It's the spirit of Las Vegas – that why-go-to-Venice-when-we-can-build-it-here attitude.

This spirit has a much more controversial side too. It is the spirit that led to European colonisation here to begin with (note – the Europeans *colonised* America, the Americans *settled* it). It's the spirit that caused the farcical election outcomes of 1960 and 2000, in which a can-do attitude is used to engineer a specific result. It's the spirit that created the current unscrupulous form of rampant may-the-biggest-man-win capitalism which America has become hated in many circles for exporting. Anything is, indeed, possible; but that does not always mean it should be made manifest. In America, there exists ample proof as to why this is the case. The spirit of America can be seen in its ability to make a shrine, not necessarily to what is there, but, as the Itasca case shows, to what America feels should be.

***

I have been bitten by the tourist bug. Hard. The bug has laid the eggs of possibility beneath my skin. The larvae of the unknown are now emerging from their fleshy beginnings, pupating into tomorrow. I want to see more. And in America, there is always more to see.

Austin, Minnesota. A dusty, one horse town so far south it's nearly on the Iowa State Line. Fields surround it. Corn fields. Wheat fields. Livestock. There are no hills – it sits square in the middle of prairie country. It would be no different from a thousand other places just like it that you've never heard of. Except for one thing. This Mecca for roadside adventurers is home to Hormel Foods – the makers of that tinned wonder, Spam. And because of this, Austin is now home to the must-see, purpose-built Spam Museum. Now this I gotta see.

We leave the Twin Cities with Gertie and some friends at about 10.00 a.m. – it is to be a long drive. It is also to be a hot drive; the outside temperature passes 110°F. It is much worse inside the car.

Less than an hour outside the Cities we begin to feel it. We need to stop to cool off. We see a sign for a Dairy Queen – which means ice cream and soft drinks for everyone else, French fries for me and my weirdo diet. As we pull into the Dairy Queen, we notice something – a shop. A big shop. A single shop about the size of an entire strip mall. Cabela's. A hunting emporium. Oohh.

My thirst having been suitably quenched with fries, we decide that it is Cabela's time. We walk in through the door. *Wow*. What a place. Every piece of hunting equipment imaginable is here. Paper shooting targets shaped like squirrels. Life-size fibreglass deer for target practice. Padded sleeveless jackets with pictures of stern-looking eagles on them that serve to turn the hunter from person into mural. And, of course, guns. There are lots and lots of guns. There are guns for as little as $90. There are guns for as much as $10,000. There are people picking guns up to try them – feel the weight, look down the barrel.

Oddly, despite owning pink underwear (pink to show I'm in touch with the Left, underwear to show that I'm still bourgeois), I do not feel any sense of revulsion or disbelief. Instead, I see people who are taking hunting seriously and, although it's not something I have ever done, it is reassuring to know that if they are going to hunt an animal, at least it is going to die as painlessly as possible. It is something. The animal gets a good life and a quick death, unlike those poor sods that are born onto factory farms – pigs that have their teeth pulled out at birth so they can be fed slop, for example. Speaking of animals, I appear to be on my high horse again.

Now, there's something else about this hunting store that makes it a must-see. Cabela's has an array of taxidermy displays, featuring scenes which could never exist in the wild. There are huge dioramas that depict, say, a polar bear with an eagle flying over its head and a kangaroo beside it. Great stuff. There are literally hundreds of pieces. And to top it all off, there is a huge aquarium – stocked mostly with local fish – but impressive nonetheless.

Soon, we need to be on our way again. As we walk out of the shop, I grab a free hunting magazine from a stand. I am interested to read points of view from the hunting fraternity. We get into the car and drove back out onto the I-35 – a road that, like the Mississippi, travels all the way from Minnesota down into the Deep South.

Sitting in the back of the car, I pull out the magazine to have a read. The feature story is a focus on how much George W. loves hunting. Interestingly, after our trip, Vice President Dick Cheney makes his one and only campaign stop in Minnesota. The venue? Cabela's.

"What did you spend $4.25 on a hunting magazine for?"

"What?"

"What did you spend $4.25 on a hunting magazine for?"

"I didn't. It was free."

Then I see it too. The price tag. I think back – I don't distinctly remember a 'free' sign – I'm not really sure what I do remember. What I *know* is that I manage to steal something from a place that has one of the largest gun safes in the Mid-West on a sunny day that brought *hundreds* of hunters to a right-wing store at a time when the American press is very anti-European. *Well done, Seán.* Not only did I once jaywalk in St Paul, but now I am a thief. Still – Austin is close enough to the State Line that I can make a run for it if need be.

One of the friends along with us today is an architect. He talks us into stopping in Owatonna, Minnesota (not far from Cabela's) to see a building, The National Farmers' Bank, designed by the great American architect, Louis Sullivan. Soon, we are in Owatonna town centre. It is a very pretty little town – one of the few smaller towns that has retained any of its original character. If Owatonna was an actress, she'd have aged gracefully and not felt the need of a face lift.

The bank is closed, but we can just about see the inside through a small window. And, in fairness, it is pretty spectacular, and well worth the stop. I always enjoy things that I normally wouldn't when there is a genuine enthusiast with me.

And we are on our way again. By now, we are driving on the county road system – endless straight concrete roads that stretch into the surrounding golden fields. After about forty or so hot, hot minutes, we arrive in Austin, and began looking for the Museum. We locate this not by following the signs, but by following our nostrils – the smell of pork wafts from the nearby factory. We are in Spam City.

The Spam Museum is, in short, fantastic. It's flashy, it's ridiculous, it's Spam. It's the best example I have ever seen of making something profoundly uninteresting (like tinned meat) interesting. There's a documentary shown every half-hour that focuses on the cultural impact of Spam rather than the boring corporate side. It includes such unlikely cultural heroes as the Spamettes – a female singing group that, well, sing about Spam. There are interviews with the people who own a Spam wagon – essentially a travelling Spam fast food take-away that shows up at concerts and festivals. There's the college kid who wears nothing but Spam T-shirts. It's all pretty weird. There are unusual facts, such as the fact that Hawaii eats more Spam than any other place on Earth. In what I can only hope is a typo in the narrator's script, I learn that the *average* Hawaiian eats no less than one and a half tins of Spam *a day!!* (It turns out to be six cans a year.)

We tour the rest of the museum. We learn about the factory and the family that started it all. We learn about the era that it comes from. We visit a factory mock-up, and get to tin our own beanbag version of Spam. We even see an exhibit based on the *Monty Python* Spam sketch. And, of course, we visit the obligatory gift shop, where I purchase a Spam toothbrush and dog collar. (Note – the toothbrush and dog-collar are merely branded with the product. A Spam toothbrush would soon prove unhygienic and would certainly fail to meet international dental hygiene standards. Also, meat is generally a poor substance for dog collars, due to persistent rumours that threaten to debunk the rampant vegetarianism of the common canine).

We leave Austin, Minnesota, past the all-Spam diner across the street from the museum, a little wiser than when we arrived. Small-town America has proven itself worthwhile yet again. We will travel home via Rochester, Minnesota, home of the famous Mayo clinic. Before reaching Rochester, where we call in to visit some friends, however, we stop for some gas. We pull in at a little diner-come-shop-come-gas station with a Dutch theme about forty-five minutes out of Austin. I go into the shop to buy some potato chips. I turn around, having completed my purchase and, as I am leaving, happen to glance up and into the diner area. There, before me, is a strange, strange sight. A man sits eating a meal at the counter. Nothing odd about that, right? Well, let me tell you about the man. Fiftyish. Baseball cap (blue) placed beside his plate. Stubble – grey, black in spots, unkempt. Denim clothing. Gaunt, hollowed, hungered look in his eyes – eyes that are, as it happens, looking right into me. A little weird, perhaps, but no more, you say? Two rosy red, smooth buttocks, defying his grey, wrinkly complexion, sit on the chair, *entirely out of the jeans!* There they are, sitting there like two rosy lords, and him just lookin' at me, holding a fork of indistinguishable food at head level – but not eating. The others see this, and begin to laugh: I am far too creeped out. Besides, it is a bad idea to piss off an obvious mass-murderer when he and his buttocks are just trying to enjoy a quiet meal. I leave the establishment, and make my way to the car – keeping a constant watch out of the corner of my eye on him – just in case. He is also keeping an eye on me – but not as subtly as I am. He looks – fork unmoving, buttocks still enjoying their day out – and stares – until I am in the car. We drive off. Safe – safe at last.

We don't stay long in Rochester, just long enough for dinner at a particularly good Mexican restaurant before moving off. There has been a threatened tornado or three. We manage to avoid them, but skirt a huge, impressive fiery storm all the way back to the Cities. It is impressive – as American storms always are. We go to bed that night, exhausted.

Although she usually does, I am more insistent than usual that Marie wear pyjamas that night. After the day just past, the last thing I need to see are more buttocks.

***

We spend the next day in the Mall of America, shopping and hanging around. We are to meet friends of friends that night in a bar in Minneapolis at sevenish. While we are getting ready, I happen to ask the name of the bar.

"Brits," replies Gertie.

"Brits? Er, that sounds like an English pub."

"Yep. Why?"

"Er, might my Irishness be an issue?"

Apparently not. Fair enough. I continue getting ready. My hair is too long for my usual style (or lack thereof), so I opt to wear it in the David Beckham Mohawk that is in style at the time.

We arrive at the pub, and make our way out to the beer garden. As we are making our way to meet the people we came to see, an arm grabs me.

"Hey look – it's David Beckham," says a drunken English voice.

I look around – a table full of English out for a few drinks.

"Sorry there – wrong country," I say in a genuinely friendly way.

Of the ten or so English at the table, nine smile. One does not.

At the Mall of America earlier in the day, we paid a visit to the massive underground aquarium. At the end of the aquarium tour, there is a 'petting pond' where it is possible to pet both Stingray and Bamboo Shark. It is quite enjoyable, and I get an 'I've petted a Shark' sticker – normally reserved for kids. I have, however, forgotten to remove it from my jacket. It does not go unnoticed by the tenth man.

"What's that on your jacket?"

"Oh – I was in the Mall of America today and came across a pond where you could pet a little shark, so I gave it a go."

"And how old are you?" he asks.

I do not really know how to respond.

"Irish wanker," he slurs, and pulls his glass back up to his lips.

His friends immediately jump up to try to calm him down. I do not want to make a scene, so I simply wish everyone a pleasant evening, and pat him on the shoulder. He grabs my hand. There is a moment, one that I – and all of his friends – want to walk away from. He has had too much to drink, and is being an arsehole, making a show of himself, his friends and his country. I snatch my hand back, smile to his friends, and walk away. For the rest of the night, he stares at me, mouthing things. It would have been unsettling except for the fact that he is so drunk, he is looking like a gobshite. He is the only truly drunken Englishman here – his friends all enjoying a social drink, him on a bender. The last I see of him – and I swear this is true – his friends are all sitting around having a laugh, ignoring him, as he runs up and down the aisles, index fingers to his temples pretending they are horns, mooing. Occasionally, his imitation lowing is interrupted by a sudden overwhelming need to tell his friends how great it is to be pissed. They politely nod before resuming their ignorance of him as he continues with his one-man cabaret.

'Typical,' I think. Ten English – nine are perfectly nice, but get a bad name because of one bad egg. Not only that, but he has also managed to give the worst cabaret performance I have ever seen.

***

There is to be another election in November. George W. Bush's remorseless spinning machine is working overtime. The opposing candidate this time – Bush having beaten Al Gore last time in the one way that Gore did not expect, namely by getting fewer votes – is John Kerry, a Senator from Boston. He seems like a decent enough guy. He isn't *that* boring – despite what the media have said about him. He seems to be up-to-scratch on the issues. Unfortunately, he has a problem – one that will not go unnoticed (although would go unsaid) in a media friendly age: John Kerry looks like a horse. Still, though. It is only June, and he has just been nominated. He has months to work up a campaign against a lousy President like George W.

Now, I was in the USA at the end of the Clinton-Gore era. I notice marked changes in the country since George took over. People just don't seem to be doing as well. I had, for the first time, seen a 'Feed the Children' campaign at a Cub Foods store – unique because it was a 'Feed the American Children' campaign – not something that would have been so in-your-face in the Clinton era. Also, Americans are being kept scared. Permanently. Twenty-four-hour news channels run constant terror alert updates. The US is running what can only be described as quasi-concentration camps at Guantanamo Bay in Cuba to hold people it deems 'enemy combatants' without charge or trial. The Patriot Act is constantly lurking over the shoulder of every citizen, looking at library books and authorising secret searches of homes. Bush's government is stripping away American liberties, all under the guise of protecting American Liberty. And he is getting away with it – because the public are scared.

This is the America that I now find in the media. But I find it curious. Initially, I think that this state exists to keep the people so scared that they would willingly do whatever the government wants – total Federal control. The more people I meet, though, the less sure I am about my initial feeling. And then it comes to me.

America was, ostensibly, founded as a result of an issue of an identity crisis with Britain. An American political culture grew up in isolation from its British counterpart. It differed to such an extent that, eventually, there was really no alternative but to break ties and allow this new culture to govern itself. Thus, without an empowered gentry on anything like the same scale of Britain, the idea of all men being equal was allowed to become mainstream to fill the perceived power vacuum. Men fought in the armies and founded the businesses that gave the new nation its economic backbone. A nation built around a common ideal.

Next came the Civil War, which resulted in emancipation for slaves.

and a re-drawing of the power lines in American politics, particularly in the southern States. What the Civil War also gave to America (regardless of the side one was on in the war) was yet another shared American experience – another common story shared by a community.

Wave upon wave of immigration followed – the Irish, the Scandinavians, the Italians, the Africans – all came looking for their piece of the pie. It had been demonstrated that it was possible to win the right to be an American through hard work and commitment to the ideals of the Republic – even if not born in America. It was, literally, the land of opportunity.

However, humans are strange creatures. Rather than create an egalitarian utopia, Americans began to organise themselves into cliques. People from different backgrounds tend not to mix well – ethnic groupings stuck together, and places like Chinatown and Little Italy were born.

This caused problems at government level. Individuals with different cultural backgrounds and different ideas on what 'power' should be now represented their own people, and had to find a way to make government relevant to them. This approach didn't work, and several groups took power. There was an emerging aristocracy who, essentially, took hold of the government – after all, that's what aristocrats tend to do in other situations. In the Italian community, powerful local families took power. In the black community, radical preachers took power. There was – and still is – a sizable community of millions of Americans who despise the notion of anyone holding too much power – a sort of 'anti-government patriot'.

And that is about where America stood on the day that George W. Bush took power, and the America that I had lived in for a time. Bush, whether actively or passively, finally gave Americans something that many of them could find common ground with – terror. The threat from fanatical terrorism now became the yardstick for being an American. Osama Bin Laden – who, perversely, has done more for a sense of American patriotism than anyone else in the post-war period

– became the yardstick. If you hate Osama, you are in.

Americans have not really had something to unite them – or, at least, a common story – since Watergate, or Vietnam. It hasn't had a positive unifying story since the end of World War II. This current generation has grown up without a positive uniting element. '9/11' provided them what they needed, in a very unusual way. The people are being kept afraid so that they will unite behind the symbols of the Republic – liberty, justice, the government. Although not a good event by any stretch of the imagination, '9/11' has been given the sense of a story itself: the bigger the obstacle, the bigger the potential triumph. People are waiting for the victory that will unite them – a victory that will have made the fear and waiting worth it. If the victory comes, it could keep the American flame burning. If it does not, another generation of antipathy towards America awaits. Bush and his cronies have declared a perpetual war. The sporadic feelings of positive patriotism experienced by Americans for the first time in fifty years could soon evaporate if those in government don't realise that the people expect a result.

This is how I find America during the summer of 2004. Terrified, yet optimistic and expectant, but with no 'results' in sight.

***

Although technically from Duluth, Marie's family lived in the nearby city (and I use the term loosely) of Two Harbors, Minnesota – a town that I have not yet visited. We decide that it would be an idea to point the car in that direction and check the place out. Smalltown America, here we come yet again.

Two Harbors, Minnesota, has a very unusual claim to fame. It is the birthplace of the 3M Corporation. To my delight, I notice that the town has what is arguably the most bizarre tourist attraction not only in America, but possibly the world – Two Harbors is home to the Museum of Sandpaper. I've read that it is, however, one of the most boring places on the continent – a supreme example of how to do the opposite of what the Spam people (figure of speech) in Austin have done. It is an uninteresting subject, boringly presented. Thus, we make a strategic decision not to seek it out – a decision reached by most other visitors to the town.

The drive from Duluth to Two Harbors is particularly beautiful. It follows the north shore of Lake Superior all the way in. Stunning. We even have the pleasure of seeing an eagle wheel around above the car on our way.

About ninety minutes later, we reach the town. It is a pretty enough little place – 'little' being the operative word. It is a tourist town, with many well-kept quirky shops – all selling combinations of wild rice, smoked fish, artisan mailboxes and agates [Two Harbors was originally called 'Agate Bay']. Indeed, I estimate that Two Harbors is to the combination of wild rice, smoked fish, artisan mailboxes and agates what Las Vegas is to gambling and glitz.

However – one of the highlights of the town can be seen just before arriving at the town centre – the Two Harbors Voyageur statue. The Voyageurs were among the earliest Europeans to live in this part of the American frontier – hairy, leather-clad hunters who trapped animals for their fur as a way to make a living. Their prominence in the early recorded history of the area has seen them become important cultural phenomena, akin to the early woodsmen and lumberjacks represented in the Paul Bunyan legends. Bunyan is an interesting character – a mythical figure – a sort of super giant-lumberjack to whom incredible feats of strength have been ascribed. Like all legends, there probably is a good element of truth to the stories. He probably was a real person, and probably was from Minnesota. He captured the early frontier spirit and, thus, when people on the frontiers (as Minnesota was for so long) told Paul Bunyan stories, they were really speaking about themselves and celebrating their way of life.

However, because of the position of the frontier in Minnesotan tradition, figures such as the Voyageurs and Bunyan are everywhere. Every small town has its statue. They are all colourful, and they are all big.

They all portray a huge, slightly portly, bearded figure with a large grin on his face – as if Santa and Rasputin had a child, and it has been working out.

Bemidji, Minnesota, is reputed to have the largest of these statues. However, by my estimation, Two Harbors has the most worthwhile. There, close to the entrance to the town, stands the smiling twenty-foot tall voyageur, dressed in his frontier style clothing. His coat is brown, and comes down to his waist. His boots are also brown, and come up to mid-thigh. There is, therefore, a gap between them – a gap in which one might expect to see some pants or trousers painted. But no. The colour they chose? Flesh. There he stands, under the Minnesota sun, thighs bared for all to see. We stop the car to get a closer look. I stand directly beneath the massive statue, looking up into his coat. Sure enough, the flesh colour continues. What makes it even stranger is the fact that the statue – like so many others – is sculpted not so much to body shape as to clothing shape. Thus, this fleshy figure has been castrated, and is missing an ass. The places in which they should have been are exposed, and although the right colour, they are absent. Not that he seems to mind, mind you, judging from the smile on his face. If Paul Bunyan's attributes were reflections of the communities that created his myth, then what does this statue of Pierre the Pantsless say about Two Harbors? I pose beneath the gigantic legs for a photo, and we are on our way.

We have a quick look through the town, see the places that are important in family lore, and return to the car. Our next stop is not within walking distance. About two miles farther out from the town, the car pulls into the parking lot of Betty's Pies. Now, Betty and her pies are a local legend. I have read in guidebooks that the pies served at Betty's are arguably the best in the country – certainly the best in the State. Ah, 'pie'. It doesn't get more American than 'pie'.

Betty's rose from small beginnings – a roadside shack where the intrepid voyageurs traversing the calamitous, unforgiving perils of the North Shore Scenic Drive would stop to get the piece of pie that stood between being eaten by the circling wolves and redemption.

Realising that trips to Betty's will probably be infrequent, I order two pieces – a slice of triple-layered mint chocolate crème pie and a slice of rhubarb and strawberry pie. It takes quite a while to come to this decision, as pie abounds. The Betty's pie menu changes daily – there are around twenty pies to choose from at any one time – half on the 'regular pie' menu, half on the 'crème pie' menu. I could go into detail on the menu – but let's just say that there is ample choice.

Soon, the waitress (who is, coincidentally, leaving to study in Ireland the next morning) returns. Pie. Hmm – lots of pie. Two *huge* pieces of pie. Feck. Either I eat all of both pieces, pretending that I know what I am doing but really wishing that Betty's would have some sort of stomach pumping service on hand (*Betty's Pie 'n Pump* for any budding entrepreneurs out there), or I attempt to eat as much as I can of each, then devour the suspiciously large slice of humble pie that comes with allowing one's head to be ruled by one's…pie.

The pies are sublime. Betty, although long dead, has outdone herself. Good pie in smalltown USA; it doesn't get much better than this.

On the way home, we pull in at Russ Kendell's for some local smoked fish. We buy some King Salmon, Cisco and Lake Trout – all caught and smoked locally. The fish is wrapped in newspaper for us to take home. That night, the day's gastronomic exploits are perfectly rounded off as we eat the beautifully smoked fish. This is the food that Americans don't export to the rest of the world – unlike scabby little Hamburgers and dry, oily little French fries – this is the real deal – the food that they keep in reserve for themselves.

***

The next day seems promising. The plan is to go to Gordon, Wisconsin, to do a little canoeing down the beautiful St Croix River – the river upon which Marie's mom is building her fancy new pad. She will be coming along – as will her boyfriend Hank. Marie and Gertie will also be in tow.

The drive there is hot – the oppressive sun beats down hard upon the Wisconsin afternoon.

The gals are dropped off at the house-to-be, while Hank (the boyfriend's name – although, admittedly, he's really more of a man-companion than a boy-friend) and I go off to get (or, rather, find) the canoes.

We take his large 4x4 and head off to one of his near-by hunting properties (the one where he uses Gummi-Bears in his bear traps – a weird sort of candied cannibalism) to get the canoes. We arrive at the entrance to the property. Hank then follows what he insists is a track through the dense forest – but that I suspect is *nothing*. Soon, whether by chance or design, we arrive at the large metal canoes. And they are infested with ants. Great.

I suck it in, however, and we manoeuvre the two…vessels onto the roof of the vehicle. We place them upside down, pointed bits at each end of the canoes pointing downward. Hank ties them off (with a little help) and I realise how long it has been since my Scouting days. We get back into our seats, and head off along the trackless track.

Bang. What the hell is that? *Bang Bang.* What the feck? The cruiser is bouncing around too much to be able to see what is going on. *Bang.* That one sounds closer. Then I see it. It turns out that the canoe which I tried to tie down has merely been tied – I had forgotten the 'down' bit. Now, the pointed bit at the stern is moving around like a giant metal beak. It is not only banging but also piercing the roof of the cruiser like a tin opener. *Bang.* Feck. Hank laughs as the roof of his dirt-mobile (no offence intended) is torn to shreds.

We arrive back, get the gals, and head off to a good launching spot beneath a bridge. Marie's mom, Hank and herself take one canoe. I am put under the charge of Gertie – usually an unassuming music teacher, but elevated to the level of fearless pirate queen for the day. Everyone else here has had at least a little experience in these things before. I have never floated in anything smaller than the Stena Sealink ferry from Dublin to Wales. I realise soon into the journey that pretending to be an old salt won't work – so I take my paddle in hand and simply relax. The cool, heavy hull of the canoe takes the edge off the hot day. The water takes us, and we glide along for a couple of hours. Wonderful. For two hours, we see no sign of Man – no cars, no people, no fast food outlets with canoe-only windows. Instead, we see eagles, fish, and even the occasional deer standing in the river – no doubt trying to hock his wares to passing travellers.

I have made sure that I am not in the ant-ridden canoe for obvious reasons. Gertie and I are first to 'weigh anchor', but the ant-mobile soon catches up. It is actually a pretty funny sight. Hank and Marie are sitting on seats at opposite ends of the boat. Marie's mom is in the middle; with no seat, she appears a good foot smaller. In fact, all that can be seen is her little head, floating bodilessly down the St Croix.

The trip ends far too soon. We stop for lunch at another of Hank's properties, and watch in horror as he catches a tick and bites its head off. (Apparently, death is a pretty good method of ensuring that the tick won't come back). We set off on the hour's drive back to Duluth. We are not five minutes on the road when we see a mother raccoon and her five babies crossing in front of us. Incredible stuff. And then I notice something...unexpected. I knew that there were bears. I knew that there were wolves. I even knew that there were bobcats and the occasional mountain lion. What I did not expect was snapping turtles – yet here they are on their annual migration in their *hundreds*. There are big ones and little ones, medium-size ones and...er, other medium-sized ones. Occasionally, we pass a particularly big one sporting a tyre-mark that has crunched through his shell as if in a cartoon – or, at least in the cartoons I watch.

***

Our trip comes to an end with the obligatory full day's travel back to Ireland – Minneapolis, Reykjavik, London, Dublin. It is equally as frustrating as the first flight, where there was just not enough time to sleep.

It is uneventful enough – although when I present my syringes to Security in the US airports, they don't even look at the paperwork – which is a little disconcerting to say the least. When I get home, out of curiosity, I look up the list of things which it is illegal to bring onto airplanes. Most of them make sense. Guns. Knives. Box-cutters. Razors. Scissors. Leaf-blowers. Leaf-blowers? I double-check the list. Yep – leaf-blowers are on the list. I think about this for a moment, but cannot get past the following questions:

1) Who brings a leaf-blower onto a flight with them?
2) Is it a common enough occurrence that it is one of the first things officials thought of when compiling the list?
3) How is a leaf-blower used as a weapon?
4) Most weapons are concealed until the moment of use
   – how would it be possible to pull a leaf-blower out
   of the overhead storage bin mid-flight and pull the cord
   repeatedly, until the motor whirred noisily into action,
   without looking suspicious?

Then again – I'm no terrorist, and have never given much thought to these things before. Maybe the common leaf-blower is the weapon of choice amongst suburban, middle-class terrorists. All I know is that I am lucky my medication is taken via seemingly inoffensive syringes – thank God that it doesn't involve sprinkling it on leaves and having someone blow them in my direction.

CHAPTER TEN

How to Order Eggs

Back home, America is on everyone's mind again. The pay-per-view ringside US Championship bout between John Kerry and George W. Bush (the current title holder) is to take place in November. Bush, detested in Europe, is getting approval ratings of around 25 per cent in European polls – surely America will listen to what its European friends have to say when choosing a leader. But then again – with 'Freedom Fries' on the menu and French cheese off it, one can never tell.

Election day. It looks like Bush will fall. One of his re-election team, Karen Hughes, even reportedly sat him down and told him that he needed to brace himself for defeat. It all seems to be going well.

As you know, I am a political junkie. I arrive back to Ireland the day before the election, having spent a weekend at a friend's wedding in Bremen, Germany. I have extended my leave from work for another couple of days so that I can watch what I assume will be Bush's defeat. I have myself set to pull an all-nighter. I buy popcorn, crisps, chocolate and caffeinated drinks, and settle myself down upon my parents' sofa for the evening. (Marie and I just moved into our new house the day I left for Germany and we have not yet hooked up the TV.)

Soon, the returns start to come in. It is looking good (from an anti-Bush point of view). There are even early reports that the Carolinas – staunch pro-Bush areas – might fall to Kerry…and then *something* happens.

The Carolinas stop counting awhile. When they resume, Bush's numbers surge. In Florida, Bush wins by a substantial margin, despite the fact that the exit polls show Kerry winning. For the exit polls to be that far out is a one-in-a-million shot. Reports are coming through of serious voting irregularities from Ohio, including poor (Democratic, pro-Kerry) areas not having enough voting machines to deal with the number of voters. This, in turn, creates huge lines which, on sight, turn many people off voting. And the media – which were in trouble for calling 'Florida for Bush' last time before the results were in, and adding to (if not creating) public confusion – decide to call 'Ohio for Bush' before the results are in. Oh – by the way – that gives him the election. It is all highly, highly suspicious.

If there is any serious public outcry, it is not heard. Instead of examining why the exit polls in Florida are so different to the results, an attack on exit polls themselves is launched. Instead of following up on the Ohio debacle, the Democrats let it go – the right-wing American media is ready to crucify them if they try it. Bush will be sworn in as President again – never having had a clear mandate and never having definitively 'won' an election. Although the American media do not cover it, the world is beginning to think that American democracy is a sham, there to be manipulated by those with the biggest machine or the biggest chequebook. George will continue his reign for another four years.

***

The year 2005 arrives out of nowhere. I complete my studies, sit my Finals in January, and get my results in February. I am finally able to turn full attention to both my disease and to our new home. In April, we spend a week with some American friends in Copenhagen, drinking cartons (yes, cartons) of cheap wine and dining at all-you-can-eat pizza buffets. When we get home, we begin to plan our next US trip. We originally thought that we would go at Christmas, as we had a few years earlier. But, for several reasons, we thought that a summer trip would serve us better.

We book our flights – once again taking a different route: Dublin–Paris–Detroit–Minneapolis.

"It is ironic," I tell Marie. Not only would we be passing through

Paris, we'd also be passing through Detroit, the Paris of the North. I get no reply.

Marie had been in Paris before. In 2000, we bought an Inter-Rail ticket, and changed trains there. That was it. At least now, she could also add Charles de Gaulle Airport to her list of been-there-done-that tourist attractions in Paris. I tell Marie to expect unbelievable arrogance and rudeness from the Parisians – something she had already heard of. I have travelled a bit in France, but can safely say that the arrogance seems to be confined to the Parisians. It's not a mean thing either – it's a cultural thing. It's simply what they do. If you accept that it *will* happen, then you won't mind as much when it does happen. Too many people visit Paris without realising this, and come back with a negative attitude of the city.

One of my first Parisian visits led me to the same premature conclusion. I was staying in Paris for a few nights before travelling on to Germany, where I was to spend a semester studying at the university in Tübingen. I struggled to a kerb with my overweight luggage outside one of the train stations in Paris, where I intended to hail a cab to bring me to my cheap, back-alley hotel. A taxi duly stopped, and I climbed heavily inside, pulling the bag onto my lap. The driver turned around, and asked me something in French. Unsure if she was asking me where I needed to go, or whether she was asking if I wanted a hand to bury the body in my bag, I used the only French phrase I knew: "No parle Français – Parle Anglais?"

Before I knew what was happening, she had forcibly ejected me from the taxi, and driven off. As far as I could tell, I had been thrown out of a taxi for not speaking French. I regaled Marie with this anecdote (for the hundredth time) as a warning.

There is not much time left before we are due to depart – a couple of days at most – when I pack my cases. I learned a harsh lesson the last time about the searing Minnesota summer heat. I did not want to make the same mistake as a year earlier – wearing jeans in 100°F weather.

This being the case, I buy several pairs of shorts – my first since my pre-teen days. I buy a blue pair and a tan pair. I get home, and try them on. Problem. My legs are white. Let me re-phrase that – my legs are so white that if I wore dark shorts in a blizzard, it would look like I was levitating. My legs are so white that I can tell racist jokes about Caucasians. My legs are so white that…well, you get the picture. Even Marie comments.

"Seán – your legs are so white."

"Oh, yeah?" I reply. "That's the sort of thing I expect to hear from a stupid Caucasian like you."

Marie and I decide that action is both needed and warranted – my legs are just too white to be let out walking in public. My options are… limited. Skin grafts from a darker person would most likely prove too expensive and painful. Lying out in the Irish sun to get a quick tan before we go would prove futile – the very phrase 'Irish Sun' itself being a paradox, unless one is speaking about the tabloid newspaper of the same name. Smearing my legs with boot-polish would mean that I wouldn't be able to sit down unless I was wearing long trousers – which would defeat the decision to wear shorts in the first place. I am running out of options.

There is, of course, one option that would probably work – but it is one that I don't really want to consider; visiting a tanning salon. However, being short of both time and options, I feel that I don't really have a choice. On the day that I finish up work for the holidays, I pop into a salon on my lunch break.

"Hi. I'm really white, and am going on holidays somewhere that I'll need to wear shorts. What do you recommend?"

The girl behind the counter smiles.

"Well, we could give you a base-tan – it would require a few sessions over a few weeks, but we…"

"Er, no – that won't work. I'm going away in two days. What about… a spray-on tan?"

"Yes. We can do that for you in another of our branches this evening."

I look embarrassed.

"Don't worry," she chips in. "You'll go into a booth and it'll spray automatically. There won't be anyone there with you spraying you down."

With that image in mind, I decide to book the tan for that evening. I go back to work – too embarrassed by what I am about to do to tell anyone. I simply run down the clock until 5.30 p.m. Tanning time.

After a short distance, I arrive at the tanning salon. I take a deep breath, and walk in, head bowed, expecting a hundred heads to turn and look at the only guy in the place – all judging me. I look up. To my amazement, I see only men. There are men in Dublin Bus uniforms. There are men who look like my brother. Even the receptionist is a man – a big Swedish-looking (but Irish-sounding) he-man.

"Please take a seat, Seán, and we'll be with you in about ten minutes."

Sure enough, ten minutes later, I am called. I follow He-Man up to the second floor, where I am led into the booth room. The booth itself stands to the right of centre. The rest of the room is a changing area.

"Have you ever done this before?"

"Er, no."

"OK – here's what you need to do. Get ready, and step into the booth."

He steps into the booth to demonstrate – just in case I don't get the concept.

"Next, you'll see a red light – a warning. You'll have six seconds before it begins. Then it will spray for six seconds. You have just one movement to do."

And with that, he demonstrates the movement, which I'm sure comes from an old Vaudeville routine. Standing on his left leg, he turns his body – including right leg, to the left – arms up like a cheesy dancer. Then, in one swift motion, he dances over to the right – right leg now on the floor.

"You need to do this eight times."

"OK – grand."

And he keeps doing it. I soon realise that he wants me to do this movement in front of him, so that he is sure I understand. So I do. And so does he. Eight times. We are only short of diving into a pool and doing a little synchronised swimming.

"Now," he says, booth routine complete, "when you come out, make sure that you take a few wipes and wipe the likes of your palms and feet. It doesn't look very well if your palms are tanned."

'Wise words,' I think.

"OK – any questions? No? Good – here's your shower cap."

He leaves.

Not wanting a tan line, I completely de-clothe. I place the shower cap upon my head, and step into the booth. Six seconds later and I am dancing my whiteness away. I step out of the booth, wait for the tan to dry, and begin cleaning my palms and feet. It takes a good five minutes. I decide that it is as good as it is going to be: time to get dressed. And that's when I notice something. I forgot to close the blinds, and have, in effect, been putting on my own naked version of a Vaudeville routine for the street below. Great. You try to do your best for America, and you're turned into a weird dancing tan-stripper.

I get dressed and go down to pay. I am told not to shower for twenty-four hours to let it develop. I will go to bed that night with that in mind.

I am looking pretty blotchy. Not to worry. I have no plans for that evening, and am not expecting company. My parents won't call and my brother – who lives a mere two-minute walk from me – never calls, so nothing to worry about there. I can be alone in my coloured weirdness. With that, the doorbell rings. I crack open the door to see who it is. My brother. Great.

"Howya Seán. I am just…What's on your face?"

I tell him the story – complete with dancing He-men. I then notice that Templeton has not come alone – a carload of his friends pulled up with him, and are calling me over.

"Howya Seán – we are just…What's that on your face?"

Out of the corner of my eye, as I tell the He-Man story to the carload of people, I can see Templeton shaking his head and looking at the ground – presumably searching for the respect that he has just lost for his brother.

The next morning, I wake with a fright. I am blotchy – very blotchy.

'Not to worry,' I think. 'It'll all be revealed when I shower off the excess.'

Into the shower I get. Soon, something very disturbing becomes apparent. I am, in fact, blotchy after all. I am particularly blotchy in several unfortunate areas, including my shins and calves, which will be showing from my shorts. And my hairline – I did not put on the shower cap correctly and now have a border crossing my forehead. But worst of all is…my feet. My toenails are coloured. I look like I have a really, really bad fungal infection. Great – and I will be wearing sandals.

***

We arrive at Dublin Airport having completed a five-week complaining stint, concerning the lengthy flight, the five-hour layover in Charles de Gaulle (I once had a terrible seven-hour layover there) and the three hour-layover in Detroit. We check in with Aer Lingus – my own personal trouble-free airline – and are on our way. The flight is to leave at 7.00 a.m. We have boarded and are ready for take off by 6.55 a.m.

'Weird,' I think. 'These things aren't usually ready in time.'

The thought came too soon.

An announcement.

"This is your Captain speaking. We're fully boarded, have our paperwork done, and are ready to go. Unfortunately, the European flight controllers have forgotten to include us on their schedule for the day, so we're going to be sitting here for a while until they can fit us in."

Great.

An hour later, the plane takes off. We are finally on our way. The flight itself is uneventful enough, and about an hour and a quarter later, we land at Charles de Gaulle. Or, rather, we land at an airport named in honour of Charles de Gaulle. We taxi our way to a waiting stairway, passing an endless stream of Peugeot and Citroen cars and vans. The plane comes to a halt. Now, in most airports, the planes empty row-by-row in an orderly, well-mannered fashion. Not so in Paris. The Irish sit in their seats, waiting for their turn to deplane. The French – sorry – Parisians surge forward like children, an unruly mob of rude French clambering over each other, as if on their way to storm a Bastille somewhere. I sit back and watch the carnage unfold with a smile on my face.

Soon, we deplane, and board a waiting bus. I usually hate these bus journeys to the Terminal – they're usually ridiculously short. I wonder if I can walk, but know better than to question a Parisian airport official. We are crammed on like monkeys into a small box. The bus pulls away. Thirty minutes later, the bus arrives at the Terminal. We go in to collect our bags and re-check in. We will be flying on to Minnesota with Northwest.

We collect our bags, and make our way to the ticketing counter. Wrong ticketing counter. Wrong Terminal, for that matter. We need to go to Terminal 2. We are in Terminal 1. Shouldn't be too far away. We exit the Terminal, and go to the inter-Terminal bus stop. The bus arrives, and we get a reminder of where we are. The driver is an elegant-looking black woman, dressed in a white skirt-suit, complete with fancy hair-do and large white bangle earrings. Welcome to Paris.

Things are not going well today. The bus trip to Terminal 2 takes a further half-hour. We are, by now, becoming worried. There are now only three and a half hours to go before take-off. We haven't even checked in yet. Arriving in the ticketing area of Terminal 2 does little to allay our fears. The queue is out of control – like a naturally large queue with unnatural silicone queue implants and an extra nipple. We stand in line, moving slowly forward. *Two hours* later, we reach the top. We race to the craft, and board immediately. The five-hour layover in Paris has barely been long enough.

After what seems like someone else's lifetime, the mighty craft lifts off. Next stop will be scenic Detroit – over eight hours away. I while away the hours watching plotless movies such as *Sahara* and reading in-flight magazine articles about how Detroit could have been Chicago. I am excited that we are on our way, though – despite the fact that two large airports have already conspired against me today.

We are served an unimpressive meal of what I presume is a little-known breed of pygmy chicken, served with mush of some description. I can picture the menu brainstorming session at the airline:

'So we have pygmy chickens and the mush. What else do we need?'

'What's wrong with a meal of pygmy chickens and mush? Sounds pretty sweet to me. We don't need anything else.'

'You raise a good point – and besides – it's just for the people in economy class. (picks up phone) Hello Tina? Get me United Mush on the phone. We need to triple our order.'

The route is familiar enough – we even fly back over Ireland, before heading up to beautiful Greenland. From there, Quebec and Lake Huron. The plane now changes direction slightly, and makes for Detroit. Motown, the city that attracted Marie's grandparents up to the Mid-West seventy years earlier from Georgia. Soon, we land, and are taxiing towards the Terminal. The Parisians on the plane have already unbuckled their seatbelts and are off in search of another Bastille.

The airport itself is brand spanking new. It is also *huge*. Great. Another big airport. That is all I need. We arrive in to the Terminal, and split up – the Immigration lines for 'citizens' and 'terrorists'. The line that I am in is full of French tourists – French people who can't speak any English. It is causing problems, as the Immigration official doesn't speak any French. He is becoming frustrated. Great. I approach, and hand in my passport.

"Where you headed?"

"Duluth."

"Duluth? What's in Duluth?"

"Er, family."

"You're from Ireland! Great! My parents are from Ireland."

Great. Here we go.

"Wow – fantastic. Which part?"

"Cork."

"Ah, Cork – European capital of culture, a beautiful place – wonderful people."

Having been made feel suitably good about himself, he stamps my passport with aplomb, and wishes me well.

I meet Marie on the other side. We go to the baggage reclaim, where the airport has employed someone to stand all of the bags on the carousel upright so that they will be easier to grab. Nice touch – is Detroit *(gasp)* a well-run large airport??

We retrieve our bags, and walk through Customs.

"Where you headed?" asks the Customs official.

"Duluth."

"Duluth? What's in Duluth?"

We re-check in, and make our way to the Terminal. Wow. A half-hour to land, deplane, go through Immigration and Customs, collect and re-check our bags! Not bad!

The airport is spotless and seems friendly enough. Alas, it would not be all smooth sailing. This is, however, through no fault of the airport. The problem is the airline, Northwest. We reach our gate – which is unusually full. Apparently there are unusually large numbers of people on stand-by. But that is not all. The airline has also decided to downgrade the plane – a fully-booked 200-seater – to an overbooked 160-seater. The staff are asking people not to fly.

"Hi! We've had to switch planes and as a result need forty volunteers not to fly. You will be compensated with a flight tomorrow, and we'll put you up in a hotel for the night. We'll also give you an open ticket, good for one year, to use anywhere in the United States."

Pretty sweet deal! Marie and I briefly think about it – the chance to see scenic Detroit and a free night – but decide against doing it as we only have fourteen days in the USA as it is.

The forty or so compensated 'volunteers', however, soon step forward. We board the craft. Everyone is actually in a good mood, and has taken this inconvenience in their stride. It is great to see, I must say. A Scout leader asks me as we are walking down the jetway where I am headed.

"Duluth," I reply.

"Duluth? What's in Duluth?"

What does everyone have against Duluth? Let me re-phrase that – what do people who live in *Detroit* have against Duluth?

Soon, we are on our way again – a mere ninety minutes from Minnesota. The flight is quite pleasant – everyone is in an unusually good mood and all are relaxing. Soon, we land in Minneapolis-St Paul International, and make our way to the Exit, where Marie's sisters and the men in their lives greet us. We then go to the baggage reclaim – which is, unusually, situated in the public area. Forty minutes later, our bags appear. *Damn you*, large airport. *Damn you to hell.*

We go to Gertie's apartment in Edina, and go to bed. We leave for Duluth in the morning.

***

It has been a hot, hot summer in Minnesota. In fact, the temperature on the evening we arrive reads 105°F. To put this into perspective, if the State was a person, it'd be lying on the sofa, damp cloth on its forehead, babbling incoherently as a nearby priest flings holy water and administers the Last Rites. I have never been to Minnesota in August – but since the snows usually start in early October, I did not expect it to be quite so warm. In Detroit airport, I bought a $4 orange plastic fan. It came highly recommended by the shop assistant – who even gave me a demonstration by blowing cool air into my face. Then again, I suppose, what else could she have used it to demonstrate?

In any case, this is the final piece of 'Operation Keep Seán Cool', a plan which Marie and I devised to counter the extreme thermotropic responses (or lack thereof) of my white, Irish body. Phase one included the purchase of shorts and T-shirts. Phase two involved the darkening of my legs – a folly which had, inadvertently, brought about the blackening of my name. Phase three involved the purchase of Rapolyte – a sachet of foul tasting powder that, if diluted, will replace the electrolytes and salts lost by the body during diarrhoea. This is appropriate, since the amount of salts and moisture lost by the body on a hot American summer's day is akin to having severe skin diarrhoea. Phase four involved having a pair of two-litre bottles of water with me at all times. All four phases are now in operation, and when we wake the next morning, I don my shorts and sandals, drink what I think is a Rapolyte (although it tastes of urine), and pack a 'day' bag that includes four litres of water and a fan from Detroit.

I enter the kitchen, where Marie and Gertie are having breakfast. Almost immediately, Gertie notices my fungal infection toenails.

"It's not a fungal infection. It's a fake tan."

I see a confused look now creeping across her face, which says 'How is that any better than a fungal infection?'

***

Outside, it is obvious that summer has overstayed its welcome. The sun beats down upon everything. Nothing remains of June except for an occasional patch of green lawn that has taken refuge beneath the trunk of a shady tree. Grass has turned a yellowed brown – dry, dusty, sparse and parched. There are few living bugs left around – which is nice for me. Instead, their dried corpses lie like fallen twigs at the side of footpaths – or squashed warmly into the pavement like chewing gum.

Exhausted trees and plants allow their seeds to fall wearily through the windless sunbeat to the ground. Hungry squirrels – the same mangy species that I saw invading the Cities five years beforehand – scamper around in the shade gathering them for the winter that is, by now, imminent.

And the sun, the sun, the heavy, tireless suburban sun – and I beneath it, as weary as the dry brown grass, already seeking respite despite my very recent arrival. America has been experiencing a deadly heat wave. Acres of the Minnesota Northwoods up around Grand Portage are aflame – the entire area dried to tinderbox over the course of the past couple of months. There will be no rain to quench them, no water to stop them. There will only be a still, scorching sun-lit sky – sucking what little moisture is left from the air, spurring on the advance of flame. It is 100°F that day – one of the coolest days in a fortnight.

Most of the roads and pavements in Minnesota are cracked and ugly – the extremes of temperature too much for human engineering to completely overcome. Makeshift, poorly installed cheap air conditioners hang precariously from open windows, their vents dirty from overuse. Occasionally, a green lawn hints at a leaky water pipe beneath. But only occasionally. Only life on the banks of the Mississippi thrives – an oasis of deep, deep green in a land of oppressive brown, dry, cracked and brittle.

Summer has come to Minnesota, and has sucked the very life from the ground. Summer has come to Minnesota. It has long since overstayed its welcome.

***

We load up the car for the three-hour trip to Duluth, and soon are on our way – Marie, her sisters, and myself. I sleep for most of the journey, but manage to wake just in time to once again see Duluth and Superior appear below as we cross the final hill on the outskirts. Soon, we arrive at Marie's mom's house in Lakewood, and unpack for a quiet, relaxing vacation.

And that is pretty much what we get. It is a vacation during which we touch base with family – all in town at the same time from places as far afield as Kansas and Saskatchewan in Canada. We play a lot of music and drink a lot of wine. OK – *we* play a lot of music and *I* drink a lot of wine. Actually, the wine is interesting. I pour myself a glass – or, rather, press upon the little tap and squirt it from the box into a glass. Fine frothy head on it. I taste it. Suspicion. It tastes too…artificial. I say nothing, however, and continue drinking. It is only a couple of days later, when the five-litre box has been tilted forward upon the fridge shelf to drain the last dregs of the Dionysian delight, that I notice something. An 'ingredients panel' printed onto the side.

'Weird,' I think. 'Wine doesn't usually come with an ingredients panel.'

I look closer. Weirder still. 'Wine' shouldn't appear as an ingredient in wine. I read it again. 'Ingredients: Wine, Water, Flavouring'. Great. True to form, however, it does not take me long to develop a liking and add it to my Irish shopping-list.

***

Into Duluth we go, to stop off at a grocery store to allow me to buy all of the weird crap on my diet. I buy a watermelon heavier than triplets, lots and lots of fresh corn on the cob, and go to the fish counter to pick up some fresh lake-fish.

"Where you from?" asks the guy behind the counter.

"Er, Ireland."

"Great – wow! Ireland." (pause) "Wanna come out on a boat?"

I don't have to think long.

"No."

Fishman then launches into an impressive tirade on catching and cooking fish. A rare employee: both enthusiastic and knowledgeable about his work.

"Want to see a picture of a pike I caught last year?"

"Er, sure."

Before I know what is happening, I am standing in the employee staff room. The notice board is filled with the usual stuff – corporate propaganda about the importance of keeping the public out of the staff room, local charity events that promise barbecue and bake sales, with pictures of Clipart black and white balloons in the corner. I picture staff and management sitting on the fence about whether or not to attend, until they see the balloons in the corner of the poster and make a calculated decision about attending. But this notice board has one extra feature. There, in the middle of the board, surrounded and untouched by everything else, is a picture of Fishman holding a supremely impressive and ferocious looking *40 lb* pike!

"I pulled that baby from an ice-hole last winter. I had to widen the hole – too big."

It is indeed an impressive spectacle, one that is worth the detour.

"It scared the hell out of my five-year-old daughter. She ran to our dog – a Golden Retriever – for protection, but when he saw the fish he ran away too."

I like this guy.

***

Following this, we meet up with some friends, and spend the evening downing a few at Sir Ben's, a nice little drinkery in Duluth.

Now, alcohol is not something I've talked much about up to now. There is a reason for this. It's not that I don't drink – I enjoy the occasional scoop – the problem is that I *can't* drink. I cannot hold it. I have far too many embarrassing alcohol-related stories for a man of my age.

I do have a drinking problem – but not the typical kind. Alcohol has an effect on me the same as everyone else – I just get there a lot quicker. I have been known to slur my speech after (or before finishing) one drink. After two drinks, I develop hiccups. Three drinks has me in the bathroom, fashioning toilet roll inserts into long points that I can thrust down my throat to induce vomiting, and attempt relief. Four drinks has me spinning – no further need for any inducer. I don't have a problem with five drinks. Five drinks does not affect me. This is because I never make it to five drinks, and therefore have no problem.

The biggest problem with this is not the drunkenness. It is not even the hangover. It is the speed. By the time I'm pissed and acting the bollox, I've only had two drinks. Thus, everyone else has not only observed, but can *remember*, my every action. Thus, although I only drink about once every four or five weeks (honestly) I get into such a state so quickly that I have become the unwitting hero of many a drinking story.

Following my MS-related diet changes, I limited my alcohol intake, and promoted wine to the position of 'Drink of Choice'. At least with wine, I figure, I know what I am drinking. This helped with the hangover, but not with the one-man campaign against sobriety. Nor did it aid the cessation of my 'bring back the vomitorium' campaign.

America has seen this side of Seán – the worst side of Seán, I might add – since I first arrived there. At Gertie's 21st in 2000, I got so bad after three drinks that I started stroking the head of a big gay man, thinking it was Marie. After two drinks in our small Portobello flat in Dublin when entertaining some American friends, I tried to light my farts on fire, failing only because I forgot that I was wearing silk underwear. As the years went by, I began to pass out long before the night had even begun – frequently falling into bed as early as 10.30 p.m.

It is at Sir Ben's that a suggestion is made to me. I am complaining of an upset stomach after *one* lousy, miserable little drink. I have tried all sorts of weird remedies and cures – but none has ever worked. My stomach is, by now, joining in the conversation. Then I am asked if I have ever tried *Gas-Ex*. Maybe the problem is simply my stomach's inability to process the gas and fumes that inevitably build up inside while drinking.

Now, this to me is hilarious. It is a private running joke between Marie and I – as a slight against American advertising – to put 'Ex' after everything to try to solve a problem.

'I have a pimple on my face.'

'You need Face-Ex.'

'The dog won't get off the sofa.'

'You need Dog-Ex'...and so forth.

The idea that there really is a product out there with a similar name has me intrigued. Immediately following our few drinks, we go to Walgreens pharmacy and purchase it.

Unbelievable. It works! I belch my way to bed that night, a happy, merry man – drunk, but not sick, in control of my body. It is such an empowering feeling – a story of man's triumph over the 21st century scourge: gas.

***

The next day, we drive to a beach in a district of Duluth called Park Point – a picturesque community of low-rise houses built upon a sandy isthmus of land stretching out into the lake. We are going to meet family.

We arrive there at 2.00 p.m. – right on time for them to show up at 3.30 p.m. In the interim, we (Marie, her sister, her mom and myself) wait at a park bench.

After about twenty or so minutes, I feel a tinkling urge. The public restrooms (not that I need a rest) are about a five-minute walk away through the parking lot. As I walk back, minding my own business, I hear something.

Splat!

I look around. What the hell was that? Out of the corner of my eye, I notice something – something grey on the road surface, about 50 feet away. I cautiously walk towards it. Suddenly, it begins to move – to wriggle. What *is* it?

I get closer still. It now begins to take on a shape. It is…a *Catfish!*

I look closer. It is a catfish without a tail – wriggling around, trying to escape death. Poor bastard! How the hell did he end up so far from the lake without a tail? There he is, writhing – mouth opening, then closing. His grey skin stripped to red where his tail should be.

A seagull lands about 20 feet away and begins walking smugly around. He has lost something. I call everyone over to see this bizarre spectacle – suggestions are made.

"Throw him back in the lake."

Can't – he has no tail.

"Throw him to the seagull."

Can't – it would probably scare him off.

The seagull doesn't seem to be anywhere near finding him, so I do what I think best. I pick up a rock, and hoist it above my head. I concentrate: this is not the kind of thing you want to mess up. Then, with a mighty *whumph*, I smash it down upon the head of the catfish. He winces, a horrific shudder, and stops moving. I am relieved – I can leave him now – he won't suffer any more. The birds will find him soon.

I look down at him one last time. Horror. He has started moving again. Shit. Not dead. Panicking, I again pick up the rock, and smash it down on his head once more. Shudder. No movement. Relief. What a horrific ten seconds that must have been for the poor animal.

And then he begins moving a third time. I can't understand it. What I do understand, however, is that I have to act fast – poor thing must be in a shocked agony. I do the only thing I can. I smash the rock down upon his head for a third time, and follow with my foot. Twisting and turning my shoe, I smush his head until there can be no doubt. A horrific little pile of red fish paste now lies on the road surface.

I return to the picnic area, looking over every now and again – it takes another half hour for the seagull to find the fish. I have, it seems, done the correct thing. I pass by the spot about forty-five minutes later. A dark, oily patch is all that remains.

***

We return to the Twin Cities – to Edina – to spend a few days with Gertie before we leave for Ireland. The trip from Duluth takes at least an hour longer than usual – we get caught in the traffic leaving Duluth's Bayfront Blues festival. Of course, the fact that we decide not to get an early start and instead spend the afternoon in Betty's Pies, Two Harbors, doesn't help things. Outside of Hinckley, the traffic stops to a crawl. It is very frustrating, until we realise why: a classic 1960s Chevy – turquoise in colour, obviously loved and cared for – has burst into flames. The Fire

Department is called out, as is a local sheriff to direct traffic. There is also a Hell's Angels biker standing in the middle of it – neither we nor he seem sure why.

Soon, we are past it – just in time to see an inspired piece of graffiti sprayed in 3-foot-tall letters on a flyover, declaring that 'Democrats' are in fact 'Dumb-o-craps'. 'Rousing stuff,' I think, 'one that might cause many Democrats to take pause and re-consider their party allegiance.'

We need to stop for gas. Hinckley is coming up – that means Tobies. Ah, what a day – first Betty's, now Tobies. Not that I can actually eat anything, such is my diet. But still…

We pull in at a gas pump. We all get out to stretch our legs. It doesn't work. Mine are still the same length. I turn to Gertie's boyfriend.

"So, Cecil," I say to Cecil, figuring he'd appreciate being called that. "Have you ever eaten here?"

Cecil looks confused.

"What – at a gas-station?"

I break into laughter. He has never heard of the legend of Tobies – a situation we quickly remedy with a custard long john and a cinnamon roll. I manage to pick up a pan of gluten-free brownies. They taste not unlike their packaging.

We spend the rest of the trip coming up with a business plan for a niche market discovered by Cecil – the combination of Pie and French fries. Thus, Cecil's Pie-n-Fry is born.

At 8.00 p.m., we arrive back to their apartment, and set up the bed. We are all tired. Gertie and Cecil have to work the next day, so we have a few drinks, have a laugh and pass it around, and go to bed.

The following day, Monday, we pass by shopping at the HarMar Mall, where I spend a few hours in Barnes & Noble, but manage to find only *one* book that fancies my tickle. Usually I find at least eight or nine. This book is interesting, though – *The Man Who Would Be King* – the story of Josiah Harlan, a Quaker who, in the mid-19th century, travels to Afghanistan and carves himself out a kingdom. He was, in fact the last American to be a king. His story – that of a man with itchy feet, convinced that he would have to leave home to be recognised, strikes a chord with me – except for one detail. We both went in search of a place – he in search of a kingdom, me in search of America. He found his kingdom whereas I found myself.

Following our excursion, during which I also purchase a photo of a Heron on Lake Superior taken by a local artist, we go to buy some wine for an evening we are to spend with friends on Johnson Street NE. Much to my surprise, I find a Minnesotan wine section at the store. I had no idea that there were vineyards here. I buy a bottle of 'St Croix' for $13. It is pretty damn good.

We pass a pleasant evening over drinks, talking with similar age friends. The conversations are usually the same. As I write this, I am twenty-seven years old. Every twenty-seven-year-old that I have met who has actually thought about it has pretty similar life views to me. The world is not ours. Going to college did little for our employability and less for our sense of work ethic. Nothing we are promised is delivered. It is now, though, that we are starting to carve our destinies. Some of us are sitting back and letting our fate be decided by others. Some of us are being more pro-active, and are trying to establish ourselves in our own rights. It is, for many, an exciting time – full of the possibilities offered by hard work and determination. For others, the hard work itself is daunting, and they are depressed, unable to understand why the world was not handed to them on a platter as promised. This is what we talk about with our Irish friends. This is what we talk about with our American friends. We come from a section that is little-represented in the public sphere – we have not chosen to be lawyers or doctors. We have not chosen to be factory workers. We are somewhere in the middle. We pass the rest of the evening making life plans – the one true skill we possess.

***

Tuesday arrives with an unusual sound in the air – the loud, deafening noise of a sawmill. Now, I am a little confused. I heard it in Duluth last week, but had assumed that it was a noise coming from a small industrial area about a mile up the road from where we were staying. I think nothing more of it – despite the fact that it is loud. To be exact, it sounded like the noise made as a saw wheel spins into a log, cutting it in two. I justified the existence of the noise in Duluth. But in Edina? This I could not figure out. Edina is far too middle class to have a sawmill.

"What's that noise?" I ask.

"What noise?"

What noise? What *noise*? The one that sounds like a lumberjack's wet-dream. The one that sounds like Minnesota is full of trainee brain-surgeons and dentists.

"Er, the buzzing, electrical noise – like a sawmill."

"Oh – that's the locusts."

I pause. I am impressed. I have never, ever heard such a loud, impressive noise coming from an insect. For that matter, I'm not sure if I have ever heard a noise that loud come from any animal – but for it emanate from insect is doubly impressive.

I never actually get to see a locust. In fact, I don't see much of anything – the ticks are all pretty much dead by August in Minnesota, as is almost everything else that can burrow under one's skin. In fact, the only dangers by this time of year are bears and the occasional coyote (the faeces, or 'scat' as the locals call it, of which we saw at the Gordon, Wisconsin property the week before).

These animals are simple enough to deal with, though, in that it would probably be easy enough to see them coming before a swarm of them burrowed into one's skin. Also, no one deserves to get bitten by an insect. I do not have similar sympathies for those who get munched to death by coyote simply because they want to pose for a Kodak moment.

Marie and I spend a pleasant, if hot afternoon walking around Edina. We go to the Edina Grill for my favourite American tradition, breakfast. I order hash browns, eggs and buckwheat pancakes.

"How would you like your eggs?"

"Over-easy."

I am chuffed. Let me explain. The first time I was in Minnesota, answered 'fried' to this question. The waitress laughed, and walked away I wasn't sure what I had done wrong, but thought no more of it. The third time I was in Minnesota, I went to breakfast with friends. The waitress asked the question. I again answered 'fried'. She thought that I was being a smart arse. A friend, realising that I was (from an egg perspective) out of my depth, jumped in and ordered 'over-easy' for me Then it is explained. When asking 'How do you want your eggs?' the waitress is seeking one of three possible responses: 'over-easy', 'over-hard' or 'sunny-side-up'. Over-easy and over-hard both indicate that the egg has been fried on both sides. The difference is in the yolk – over-easy being runny, over-hard being, well, hard. Sunny-side-up means that the egg is fried on one side only, and is still runny.

The fourth time I visited Minnesota, we went to the Modern Café, a nice little breakfast place in Minneapolis. Again the waitress asked, again I forgot, again the same friend rescued me. This trip is different. As if fluent in American egg language, I answer 'Over-easy'. She jots it down, and I get the order. Another step towards holding my own in America. Being the foreigner, the temptation is always there to play on it, and order in one's own language. However, I am not sure how well 'Giz an egg 'r I'll bleeden' burst ya' would have gone down.

Egg-time over, we go out to look for a bank to change our emergency Euro into Dollars. We go to the TCF bank.

"Sorry – we don't deal with foreign currency."

We find this frustrating, but move on to the next bank – a US Bank.

"Sorry – we don't deal with foreign currency."

We move to the only other bank we can find – a Bank of America.

"Sorry – we don't deal with foreign currency."

She goes on to tell us that the Airport bank is the only bank *in the State* that can help us. The best she can offer is to have us open an account, deposit the money, and get a US Dollar conversion – which would take about a week. Er, no thanks. Credit card time.

We walk home through the searing, searing heat. We have made plans to go out tonight – our last night. And besides, I need a nap – the heat is all too much.

***

I get a couple of the 'What's On' guides. It does not look good: Tuesday nights do not have a lot to offer. Line dancing is an option – but I don't fancy going to anything that sounds like a Texas cocaine party. There is an 'experimental' Death Metal band playing in a bar across town. A fleeting interest with Death Metal when I was seventeen means that I know that even with a pipe-organ and fifty screaming monkeys on stage, Death Metal can never be considered experimental. It is code for 'This band sucks'. Next please. An evening of country music – sounds promising – but will it be any different to the Death Metal? In fact, Death Metal and country music frequently share lyrics – the only difference being that one is essentially an easy listening version of the other. I fancy a good hoedown however. In fact, I haven't had one since the last time I downed my hoe. I am, however, the only one who even considers this to be a valid option – particularly since it begins at 7.00 p.m. and finishes at 9.30 p.m.

In the end, we settle for an evening amusing ourselves. This should be no problem for me, as I spent most of my pimply teenage years amusing myself and have become quite adept at it. The venue we settle upon sounds promising, however – the Kitty Cat Klub in Dinkytown. I am not really sure what to expect from a place called the Kitty Cat Klub, but I eventually narrow my expectations down to either a place in which I'll have to wear a zoot suit, full of strippers and models dressed in leather catsuits (the bar – not my suit), or a place where women in their fifties go in ill-fitting cotton T-shirts with images of smiling, large-eyed kittens to organise bake-sales for charity and charity for bake-sales.

But it will be a few hours before I find out. This is because we have booked into a photo studio to get a proper family portrait taken: the three sisters and the men in their lives. Sounds daunting, doesn't it?

The last time I had my photo taken professionally was at my graduation from college. I was handed a gold-painted toilet roll insert with a red ribbon around it, and instructed to pretend that it was my degree. Little did I realise that there is little difference between the two in actuality. It was before the graduation ceremony and although the snaps turned out well, it all seemed a little dodgy. As we approached the hall in Maynooth where my degree was to be conferred, a man appeared out of nowhere – suit trousers too small, white socks protruding, thin moustache, curly black hair.

"Want to get your picture taken?"

"Er, I'm not sure."

Then, without prompting, he opened his jacket and flashed example photos that he had pinned to the inside.

Surely this American would be more professional than my last, albeit Irish, experience. We arrive at the studio – itself in a large strip mall. As we wait, I look at the pictures hanging on the wall. They are all of… babies. There is a baby dressed like a flower that some might think cute, but to me it looks like the baby is being eaten by a carnivorous plant of some description. There is a baby dressed in white linen, positioned beside a fake Greek column. It looks like the first in a series of cheap, highly illegal porn pictures. There is a baby on a bed of petals that looks as if it has been mistakenly swept up when the back yard was being cleaned. This does not bode well. I am just about to ask if anyone else has noticed the infantile theme, when the photographer appears.

"I don't usually do groups – usually just babies."

Hmm.

We go into the studio. Sure enough, it is not really big enough to cater for all six of us. That does not stop her from squashing us all together and snapping about fifteen shots. It is actually a surreal experience in many ways, particularly the fact that she keeps breaking into a leprechaun-style Irish accent, insisting that it's not something she is in control of. Weird, weird stuff.

The main idea behind the picture is to use it as a gift for my mother-in-law for Christmas. The final picture looked pretty good – except for one small thing. The couples had been switched. Ann and Sam are together: nothing odd there. However, Gertie is resting on my shoulder, and Cecil is looking a little surprised to have been paired off with Marie. For me, the odd thing is that Marie and I have never had professional photos taken of us – not even a wedding photo. Now, however, the only professionally taken 'couple' picture in which I feature has me, essentially, posing with another woman. Hmm.

This is, however, stretching it a bit, as the photographer does manage to talk Marie and I into posing for a picture by ourselves. Not being the world's most photogenic person, I agree on one condition – that I get the fake Greek column. The resulting photo looks ridiculous, depicting both Marie and I peeping out from behind the plastic column. Although we are both smiling, it is obvious that I am the only one not faking it.

The photo-shoot over with, we leave, and head to the Kitty Cat Klub (via Chipotle, of course). In we walk, and proceed directly to the bar. I pop a *Gas-Ex* before ordering a Margarita. It is a pretty nice place – a sort of Turkish harem meets the 1920s. It is the sort of place where a fake plastic Greek column would not look out of place. To my initial delight, there are no bake-sales or kittens. Great. I then look at the staff. They look far too headstrong and feminist to be strippers. In fact, they look far too headstrong and feminist to even be *asked* if they are strippers. I think better of it. Besides – we are almost out of money. I have nothing to stuff into a g-string besides *Gas-Ex* tablets and the ticket stub for my photo. I guess what they say is true. Sometimes it's hard to find a stripper.

The rest of the evening is very pleasant. More friends arrive to join us, and before long, what was to be an intimate gathering of four becomes a fully-fledged hoo-ha of ten. I go to bed that night, a little drunker than I left it that morning.

***

Wednesday. Home time. Ann has kindly offered to drive us to the airport to catch our flight. We pack, ready to face yet another nineteen hours of flights and large airports. Gertie has printed off the directions to the airport and left them on the coffee table.

Soon, we are on our way – Marie and I reading the directions, Ann following them. Left, then right. Straight for approximately 2.34562789 miles – then right again. Soon, the airport is in sight. Good. Almost there. Left. Straight. Great – planes behind a chain-link fence. Must be close now. Right. On for 207 yards. Hmm – has anyone else noticed that we seem to be the only car here? Oh – right again. More planes. Hmm – those don't look like commercial jet liners. Left here. Wait a minute – aren't they…military aircraft?

Before we know it, we are in the parking lot of the administrative centre of a military air-base. Shit – and me a foreigner. We stop. A man in uniform approaches us. Realising that now would be a poor time either to run or to fake an American accent, I step from the car. My *Herbie* T-shirt seems to calm the uniform a little, and he smiles. In my best Irish accent, I tell him that we are lost, and looking for the International Airport. He produces a photocopied, hand-drawn map, and gives me very direct instructions – including the line that our 'ETA at the Terminal will be in five to seven minutes'. We turn the car around, and leave.

Soon, we are back on the freeway. The airport is in sight again. Great. Almost there. Almost…where has the airport gone? I look behind me – there it is – behind the car, getting further and further away. Wrong turn? How will this affect our ETA?

We correct our mistake, and are soon in the Airport itself. We get out of the car, remove our luggage, and say our goodbyes. We check in, and go through the gate.

The next nineteen hours are a bit of a blur. Nothing really exciting or noteworthy happens. Before we know it, we arrive in Detroit, trying (unsuccessfully, as it happens) to purchase a bottle of Jack Daniels Reserve from the Duty Free. We board the Northwest craft on Wednesday. By Friday, Northwest are on strike. Four weeks later, they have filed for bankruptcy. Looks like we made it just in time.

I spend an uncomfortable eight hours trying to sleep. I think that I manage about an hour – but am not really sure. A man – looking not unlike an out-of-shape Ed Harris – sits in the seat across the aisle from mine. He is dressed in a pair of red shorts that inflate ever so slightly when he stands up to fart. I doubt that he had ever been to Europe before. Paris will be a shock for him on his big retirement trip

Before I know what is happening, we touch down in Paris Charles de Gaulle on a mild September morning at around 11.00 a.m. Three hours later, we have boarded the Aer Lingus flight back to Dublin, having spent a tedious hour in the shabby, uninspiring waiting area assigned to Irish flights. The room is filled with familiar accents, all complaining about depressingly familiar subjects. The weather is crap back home. The food in France is terrible. The people are so rude. Great. Four hundred miles from Ireland and home already. I wonder if any of them know that I have just spent a fortnight in Minnesota?

The plane touches down in Dublin at around 5.00 p.m. A few of the Irish on board applaud. The French look around wonder why. We are home. Grey clouds. Low sky. As the plane comes to a halt, the Parisians spring to life, surging forward in a crazed mêlée.

My father collects us from the airport and drives us home, filling us in on what we have missed during our absence. When we arrive home, our dog goes berserk – insanely happy to see us. She manages to do all of the tricks that we have taught her both spontaneously and simultaneously in order to show us what a good doggy she is. She manages to sit, lay-down, dance, give the paw and shake intensely – which is not a trick she picked up from us, but it seems to go down well with the rest of the routine. She has not had a great couple of weeks – the day before we went, we managed to re-home my brother's dog, which we had been looking after for three months while he sorted out the selling of a house. The dog – a beautiful, beautiful one-year-old German Shepherd – had become the sexual plaything of our dog – despite the fact that they are both female. Thus, with both the Shepherd and ourselves leaving her within twenty-four hours, she had the hump, and had been a grump – or, at least, more of a grump than she usually is – for the past two weeks.

The Irish accents in Paris prepare you. The low grey Irish sky viewed from the runway makes the holiday slip away that little bit further. It is not, however, until I have to wipe cold dog slobber from my hand that I truly know that I am home.

CHAPTER ELEVEN

So What Have I Learned?

America is always with us. Its stories are always in the news. Its celebrities are always on our TV. It is both a product of the world's aspirations and a product of itself. All it offers is hope. Yet hope is not enough. In August 2005, the world looked on as the American government failed people in New Orleans in their hour of need. It took days for George W. Bush to even realise there was a problem, it seemed, so focused was he on doling out reconstruction contracts to his crony friends. More so than September 11, more so than the fiascos in Iraq, Somalia and Vietnam, more so than the phoney election of 2000, Hurricane Katrina showed that the American Dream is just that – a dream – an unrealised reality wished for by the millions of poor Americans who live on family incomes of just a few thousand dollars a year. This is the America that I, in part, came to find out about.

The fact is that America promises all but delivers little. It is the promise itself, however, that keeps the status quo. If you upset the apple cart, you will lose out. Things might be bad now, but the possibility of things being better (and worse) exists. The existence of poverty in America is justified in the American subconscious through the promise itself – if the promise exists, then the possibility of people taking control of their own poverty and breaking out of it exists.

America is a hero-worshipping nation – a hero being defined as someone who overcomes adversity to achieve against the odds. Popular culture is full of stories of rags-to-riches. Thus, on some level, the 'haves' believe that the 'have-nots' should be able to make it on their own. Hence no real National Health Service, for example. Triumph over adversity is so in-your-face as a concept that people will literally do whatever it takes to triumph – thus, much is classed as 'adversity' in order to allow each member of the populace to potentially have something to overcome. This explains the huge murder and injury rate – the basic 'Love Thy Neighbour' command has been forgotten by many. This, in turn, explains the huge 'religion industry' in America – a genuine attempt by so many to reconcile these incompatible differences – the huge cultural influence of finding adversity to triumph over, and the huge religious influence of 'love thy neighbour'. This religious overcompensation for the cultural binge then explains the massive sweep of political ideologies from extreme right to extreme left. One side turns to their faith to look for answers to the ills of society, others try to look at society itself and see fervent religious belief in the wrong light. Instead of seeing it as an attempt to solve the problems of society, it is seen as an unrealistic attempt by the right to impose their religious rules – rules that do not seem to have any basis in American reality. Each side fails to see that the other genuinely has the best interests of America at heart. And instead of an enlightened dialogue between the two sides, petty, meaningless squabbles are played out in a media that lives too much for the moment to realise that there is even a debate there at all. Instead, the media pick up on stories about displaying the Commandments on public lands and the fact that States in the Southern USA are banning sex-toys – all symptoms of a problem that the media has yet to realise. Every four years, these differences are crystallised as a warrior from each camp does battle – Democrat and Republican. No matter who wins these contests, the victor rarely acknowledges the problem and, instead, thinks that his or her camp is the flavour of the month, and the camp to be pandered to.

It is the ignorance of the problem that has led to so many being able to talk about problems that they cannot overcome. The fear of failing to overcome a problem feeds a lucrative psychological services market, a protected environment in which one can admit failure and move on: the chance to manufacture and deal with adversity in a controlled environment. It also means that it can be very difficult to talk about unsolved problems outside of such controlled environments. For example, I've noticed that in Minnesota, a problem is not a 'problem' unless it is talked about – and there are no problems in Minnesota.

The American Dream is both the making and breaking of a great society. Teddy Roosevelt gave the dream a reality when he claimed that his vision for the realisation of the dream was for each citizen, regardless of race or creed, to get a 'Square Deal'. It was a noble idea, and a genuine, if unconscious, attempt at redefining what America fundamentally stood for – still the Land of Promise, but where all that was needed to be taken seriously was to be an American. Nowadays, that idea is dead.

Interestingly, the media 'overcoming adversity' frenzy still continues – but the adversity is now, amazingly, becoming self-defined. Rather than actually having to look for and achieve the dream, everyone has now been invited to the American Dream party. The goal is no longer to actually overcome adversity in a traditional sense. Instead, one merely needs to tell a story that casts one in this light to be offered a place at the table. America appears to be missing the sense of sacrifice and community that comes by truly honouring the 'love thy neighbour' command as a result of this. Thus, America overcompensates by sending armies off to fight more wars than are necessary – the armed services being one of the few outlets where one can achieve a true sense of sacrifice. Interestingly, the wars themselves appear to be fought against a righteous ideological backdrop – whether it's overtly stated or not. Thus the army provides an all-you-can-eat, buffet-style ready-made sense of sacrifice and adversity to overcome, for those who will never get a chance to overcome other things such as their poverty.

***

This book is based on my experiences in America and what I believe I have learned as a result of them. In essence, I learned that America is an idea. Once you can get past that, it has the same flaws and the same problems as everywhere else. I experienced America through Minnesota

— a fairly typical, slightly liberal part of the country. But, then again, America is too big a place to ever experience all of it.

I will go back to America. I will find out new things about the country — things that will challenge ideas that I take for granted. I will find that I am right about some things about America, and wrong about others. I will meet new people and keep up old friendships. I'll collect new stories.

What I'm trying to say, I guess, is that America keeps changing — there are new concepts, stories, legends and characters added to the idea of America every day. And because of this, the 'America' that I found is my own. It's not an experience that anyone else could have. It is now that I finally come to a sense of what America is:

America can be anything, America can be everything, America can be nothing. For us all, it exists in our own thoughts and notions. It exists in our own personal American Dreams.